a gift from the Author
with message next page

My Mother
Gave Birth to Me Twice

Dr. Aaftink

Allways remember you are
exactly where you need to be!

Thank you with all my
heart !

Martha

—See p. 80/1

My Mother
Gave Birth to Me Twice

Martha Schlender

Rev. date: 06/11/2015

marthaschlender@gmail.com

To order additional copies of this book, contact:
Xlibris
1-888-795-4274
www.Xlibris.com
Orders@Xlibris.com
716795

Contents

Trying To Remember.. 1

My First Encounter... 4

Kindergarten 5

We Fled 8

Premonition... 14

We moved to the West... 18

Bad Segeberg Refugee Camp... 20

Our new Home... 23

Lammy 26

Some memories just did not fit in 29

First Steps 33

I stopped fighting.. 35

Another step 38

Free Will 42

Soft Voice 43

My Search began.. 48

We came to Canada 51

Sugar Beets... 54

Moved into Town.. 57

My first Date 58

Post-traumatic Stress 62

I stole my one and only Photo 64

My first tea cup reading 66

My second tea cup reading 68

UFO Sighting 69

Are we being watched? 71

We are not alone 75

Cats are the Protectors of our Souls 77

Electric treatment for my body 79

My first spiritual healing 80

Be careful what you ask for 82

Oh my aching back 85

While my body sleeps 88

Shooting through space 90

What is Time? 91

The Magic of Meditation 93

Back to School 98

Raised in a nest of Scorpios 102

Astrology 103

My crown chakra opened 106

Distant viewing 107

Sending and receiving messages 109

Uninvited Guests 112

Living a Double Life? 114

Still asking for help 117

Wedding Invitation 118

My Gift from God 120

My other Reason for Living 124

Totally delighted 127

All done 130

Hysterectomy 132

The lady has aui aui 134

My Grandmother 136

Souvenirs from Siberia 139

Why? 141

Lost in Grandma's Garden 143

I still love Gardens 145

My first reading at the Nanaimo Spiritual Centre 146

My father's father 152

You need to write that book 154

We exist forever one way or another 157

My Dearest Childhood Friend 161

The gift of laughter 166

Can we stop our pain? 169

A quick trip to Victoria 171

About the Book 175

About the Author 177

I dedicate this book to my Hero

My Mother

Trying To Remember

"How old was I when that happened?"

"How old was I when that happened?"

Ever since I was a little girl I asked that question whenever we talked about family memories. It seemed to be the most important thing I ever wanted to know. I did not understand why I could not fit them in with all my other childhood memories. I had many. My first one happened before I was one year old. I could not walk yet. We were all gathered around in the kitchen waiting for supper to be served. I was sitting in my highchair at the end of the table with my spoon in my hand. My brothers and sister were hanging out at the other end of the table to my right and Mom was at the stove preparing the meal. As I was watching them I realized that my brother had a name and excitedly pointed my spoon at him and announced:

"Blam"

"Blam."

Everybody was looking at me and laughing. As I looked at my spoon I realized it too had a name. I held it high up into the air and told them:

"Labam"

"Labam."

Again everybody laughed. I repeated this several times until no one was paying attention to me anymore. I just sat there wondering what else I could do to get their attention back. I felt left out and ignored – I did not feel happy!

My brother's name is Waldemar and the German name for spoon is Loeffel. The sounds I made were solid words to me. Babytalk. As I got older I realized that was when I grasped the concept of communication even though I was unable to pronounce and repeat words as everyone else did. The words I used were real. I now knew how to communicate except the words I used were only understood by me.

Some of my other memories happened when I was a little older. Around the age of two and a half my Mom took me next door to visit our neighbour. My friend Raitscha was playing with me and our mothers were standing in the kitchen talking to each other. For some reason Raitscha started beating up on me. I knew hitting back was not allowed so I waited until she was finished hitting me and

I got up off the floor to go get a pat on the back from my Mom because I had been a good girl. I put my arms around her leg and tried very hard to explain what had just happened. Instead of being told what a good girl I was my Mom pressed my head against her leg and told me:

"Not now!" "Not now!"

I was devastated! Many years later I asked my mother if she remembered that? Oh yes, she remembered it well. She had gone over to the neighbor's house to figure out what they needed to do to stay alive. It was 1940 and all non-Polish people were considered to be enemies no matter how many centuries they had lived in Poland.

A short time later we were ordered to pack up and move to East Germany. I remember the trip from the house to the train station. It was dark outside and raining cats and dogs. We were escorted by a man in uniform who carried a gun over his shoulder to protect us. He was soaking wet pushing his bike alongside the wagon and chatted with us and treated us to a handful of candy now and then. I don't remember the train ride but remember arriving on our new farm in East Germany. After that my memories were really steady.

My First Encounter

I was about five years old, lying in bed trying to fall asleep when I noticed something move on top of the dresser beside my bed. When I turned to have a look I saw a giant grasshopper, I really mean giant grasshopper, sitting there looking straight into my eyes. He must have been at least eighteen inches tall and eighteen inches wide. That scared me momentarily and I lifted my arm to hit him as hard as I could to make him go away except half way through my heroic move I changed my mind. He was still looking straight into my eyes and did not seem to feel threatened. He was beautiful! Absolutely beautiful! I was in awe and no longer scared. I just lay there gazing right back at him until I fell asleep. It never happened again and many years later I told myself that had been one of my spiritual guides.....

Kindergarten

Around this time I was old enough to go to Kindergarten. I was the first child in my family who had that opportunity. This was a big day! My mother packed two hard boiled eggs and a facecloth for me and walked me down to the school. It was probably one and a half kilometer from our house. We passed two farmhouses, some open fields, another two farm houses, another stretch of open fields and the town was in sight. It probably was not that far away but when you are only five years old it is quite a hike. When we arrived my mother introduced me to the teachers and left. I do not remember what we did that morning but I will never forget lunch! After washing our hands and faces we sat down in the dining room. We each had a plate in front of us filled with potato salad, vegetables and two broken up hardboiled egg whites. Those were the egg whites I had brought with me that morning! Where were my egg yolks? What had happened to my egg yolks? They had stolen my egg yolks! I was terribly upset! After lunch we had to stretch out on a cot, close our eyes and have a nap. I never had naps at home and was not too happy to be lying there doing nothing. Every time I opened my eyes to see what was going on I was told to shut my eyes and keep them shut.

The afternoon finally went by and my Mom came to pick me up. The next morning the same thing happened. Mom gave me my little bag with the two hard boiled eggs and a fresh face cloth. Since I now knew the way nobody walked with me. I was on my own. I found the place all right, went inside, handed over my bag of goodies and went on with my morning. Lunch time finally arrived and to my surprise I did not see the egg yolks on my plate. The two egg whites were there but the yolks were missing again. I was not happy! After lunch we had to have that nap again and again I was not allowed to open my eyes.....

On the third day the routine was identical to the first two days. I had it – I did not belong here! When my Mom handed me the bag the next morning I went out the back door as usual but instead of walking outside I turned to my left and crawled under the staircase in the porch where everybody dropped their dirty farm boots and shoes before entering the kitchen. It was pitch dark down there. There was no electricity because at that time we were using petroleum lamps inside the house. I made myself comfortable and just sat there. When I thought it was time to have lunch I took my two eggs out of the bag, peeled them and ate them, egg yolks and all! I had a good day. Later that afternoon I crawled out of my hiding place and entered the kitchen like I had just come back from Kindergarten. The next day I did the same thing. I had no complaints. All was well. On the third day I had my routine down pat but after having my lunch I had to rearrange myself, my butt was hurting from sitting on some boot or shoe the wrong way. Just as I rummaged around down there my mother opened the outside door and as she came into the porch she heard the noise under the staircase.

She bent down and stood there looking straight at me with the most unbelievable look on her face.

"What are you doing down there! You are supposed to be in Kindergarten!"

After getting out of there I had to tell Mom what has been going on these last few days. I told her that they stole my egg yolks and then I had to lie on the cot forever with my eyes closed. Of course I did not mention that I was also served potato salad and vegetables every lunch. That did not seem to be of any importance to me. Mom tried to convince me to change my mind about attending Kindergarten but no matter what she came up with, I knew I would never go back there again. Mom gave in and told me it was all right; I could stay home.

Our farmhouse was quite large but the kitchen, family room and dining room were all combined into one large room and five children and Mom and Dad filled it up a little too much for my liking. When friends dropped by to visit it seemed a little much for me so I would hide out under the dining room table. I loved sitting under the dining room table. It was covered with a large table cloth and it felt like I was in my very own world. I did not do anything specific. I just sat there with my mind drifting and wandering..... I would lose track of time and became detached from my surroundings. Very much like sitting under the staircase!

A seeker of silences am I
And what treasure have I found in silences
That I may dispense with confidence?

Khalil Gibran

We Fled

In the evening of January 27, 1945 at ten o'clock we were listening to the radio. Hitler was giving a speech about the progress they had made during the day invading areas in Poland and repeated himself again and again: 'Victory is ours!' - 'Victory is ours!' In the morning at four o'clock I woke up with a start because someone was knocking on my parents' bedroom window and desperately shouting:

"If you want to live, get out! The Russians are coming!"

Within minutes the whole household was up and preparing to leave everything behind. My job was to get dressed and pack everything that was important to me. I took my amber headband and matching bracelet outside and smashed them against the wall. Again and again until the pieces were so small that no one would pay any attention to them! If I could not keep them the Russians would not get them either! My older sister, who was twelve years old, was told to dress our little baby brother nice and warm. When Mom went to see how she was doing she saw my little baby brother dressed in every piece of clothing he owned. He could not move. He lay there on the bed looking like a huge stuffed teddy bear. A few hours later we were ready to leave. Mom had managed to get everything of importance packed and stowed away. My baby brother, my little sister and I were tucked away in the middle of the wagon between our down quilts and pillows.

We said goodbye to our home, our farm and our life the way we had known it until then. I loved the huge flock of turkeys my Mom kept behind the fence beside the barn. Whenever I got dressed up in my little pink fur coat I would sneak out and aggravate the turkeys until I was told to stop it. We had a lot of chickens, geese, ducks, pigs, cows, horses and of course our dog. We would never see them again.

We were on the road day after day moving west. As we progressed we met up with more and more wagons and after a few days we could see covered wagons all the way ahead of us and behind us as far as we could see. The next few evenings when we stopped for the night we ate the food Mom had packed for us. We each got a piece of frozen home baked bread and a piece of frozen butter. As long as the milk lasted we also got a chunk of frozen milk. A few days later we had run out of milk and Mom would lift me off the wagon as soon as we arrived in a village where we would spend the night and give me my baby brother's milk bottle. She would show me a street and point out a few houses where I was to go and knock on the door and ask if they could give me some milk for my baby brother.

Some of the households did not have any milk but most of them asked me if I had eaten yet. Sometimes they would give me a bowl of soup to eat and some would make me a sandwich. I went from house to house until I had a bottle of milk for my baby brother before I would turn around to go back to find our wagon. A few times I walked past our wagon without recognizing it and my older sister would come running after me to bring me back to my family.

One evening as I walked around the corner I came to a large stone wall and stopped at the gate to watch the commotion. At the far end of the yard were about a dozen of soldiers in uniforms and one man in civilian clothing screaming and crying and fighting off the German Shepherd dogs which were attacking him. The soldiers were watching and directing the dogs to keep attacking the civilian. He fell down to the ground a few times and the dogs kept biting his arms and legs until he stopped screaming and moving. At this point I was too scared and too confused to do anything but run on to find my wagon. I had just watched a man getting killed by a couple of dogs but did not tell anyone about it.

My Mom apologized to me and explained that I was the best one to go out and ask for milk. My brother was three years older and would have been more capable of doing the job but boys don't do well when it comes to begging. A couple months prior I had just had my seventh birthday.

We had been on the road for about a week or so when we decided to stop and take a rest. We had run out of food. Everyone was getting sick and our horses and wagon were stolen over night along with some of our personal belongings. A farmer took us in and supplied us with a room on the upper floor. A few days may have passed which I don't recall but the next thing I remember the Russian airplanes started flying overhead and dropped bombs all around us. A French soldier, who also took shelter on that farm, showed up out of nowhere and took all of us downstairs to the basement of the barn and showed us how to stay safe during the bombing. He did not speak any German and none of us spoke French. He took us over to the basement window and told us to pay attention to the direction the planes were coming from. If they came from the west we were to run to the west side of the room and squat on the floor as close to the wall as possible and to the east side of the wall if the planes came from the east. We followed his directions until the bombings were over. We were lucky, none of the bombs fell close enough to hurt us.

A few days later I was hanging out on mainstreet when I noticed a long line of Russian tanks coming down the street. I stopped and watched them drive past me. Each of the tanks had a soldier sitting on top with his upper body sticking out of the opening holding a machine gun ready to shoot. I saluted every tank that passed me, in Russian, and all the soldiers seemed friendly and returned my greetings. As soon as the last tank was out of sight I ran home and told my mother.

The next three days that followed were total chaos. The soldiers were allowed to ransack any home and take anything that interested them. They did a lot of damage everywhere they showed up. We were totally helpless. I remember my mother asking all of us children to kneel down on the floor in the middle of the room and she knelt beside us with her arms stretched out all around us. The first group of soldiers that came into our room just stood at the door watching us and my mother started to

talk to them in Russian. I still remember her voice. I had
never heard fear in her voice before then and since then
I have never been able to forget it! The soldier in charge
stretched his arms out and held the other soldiers back
from coming in. He told my mother she would have to find
a good hiding place if she did not want to get raped and
to take my oldest sister, who was twelve years old, with her.

After they had left the French soldier showed up and took
us to the farmyard where he showed my mother where she
could hide out for the next few days. What I could see was
an area of about eight by ten feet or maybe nine by twelve
feet wide holding the dirty straw and hay that was cleaned
out of the pig sty and cows manure piled up until it was
hauled away to fertilize the fields. He went over to one
corner and lifted a ten-by-ten post and pushed it aside.
Underneath I saw a huge, perfectly square area finished
in cement walls about one meter deep. It was filled with
rainwater that had washed through the manure filled straw
and hay lying on top. It was only a few inches deep but
smelled so terribly bad I almost choked on smelling it. He
found a wooden box lying nearby and dropped it into the
opening and pointed at my mother and sister to get down
there and sit on the box whenever they needed to hide.

Before they disappeared into that hole my mother told me
to go play by the gate and watch the street for oncoming
soldiers. I was told to pretend that my mother had died
in a bombing and that I was on my own. Several times
during those three days before the soldiers could even ask
me where my mother was I would be playing and skipping
around and start speaking to them in Polish. They were
taken off guard and started conversations with me wanting
to know where I came from and, of course, where my
mother was. I would start to sob and tell them my mother

had died when the bombs started to fall and I no longer had a Mom now. They would pat me on my head and take off as soon as they could. Mission accomplished – they did not want to listen to my sob story. I would tell my mother when the coast was clear so they could come out of their hiding place.

I object to violence
Because when it appears to do good,
The good is only temporary;
The evil it does is permanent.

Mahatma Gandhi

Premonition

WW2 had ended and we now were refugees living under Russian government in East Germany. Things had settled down some. My grandmother was living with us. One afternoon I was sitting on a foot stool playing while my grandmother was busy changing clothes behind me. Suddenly the head of Sterna, one of our cows from back home who had a star on her forehead, showed up right in front of my face. She was slightly transparent. I pushed her head and boldly told her to go away. My grandmother asked me what had happened and looked quite worried when I told her.

Many years later I learned that seeing or dreaming of cows foretells of sickness. Sterna came to warn me because not long after that happened I became seriously ill with diphtheria. My little baby brother died after being sick for a few days and my four year old sister got well after a week or so.

I was in a coma most of the time but I could see and hear everything that was going on around me. I had no pain. I felt like I was wrapped in a soft, warm cloud. One time a neighbor came over with a bowl of soup for me. She sat down on the edge of my bed and reached over to touch me. My mother grabbed her arm and said:

"No! No! Don't touch her. If you touch her she will die!"

I felt sad that Mom was so upset with me dying. Dying had nothing to do with me but I did not make an effort to tell her that. I felt like I was in a world of my own and felt quite disconnected from them.

Some time after that Mom and my brother took me to town to the hospital. It was the middle of winter. About half way there I heard Mom say to my brother:

"Stop the horse. Stop the horse. Let her die in peace."

> For what is it to die
> But to stand naked in the wind
> And to melt into the sun?
> And what is it to cease breathing
> But to free the breath from its restless tides,
> That it may rise and expand
> And seek God unencumbered.

> Khalil Gibran

It was a beautiful sunny day. The sky was an incandescent blue and not a single cloud anywhere in sight. Again I felt like I was wrapped in a soft, warm cloud and had no pain and all the way to the hospital I was watching the wheat fields along the road abloom with red poppies, daisies and bachelor buttons.

Years later my mother told me I was having severe convulsions and my body was thrashing uncontrollably when they stopped the horse to let me die in peace.

When we arrived at the hospital we were told it was filled with wounded soldiers and no civilians were allowed in. All Mom could do was turn around and take me back home. The horse Mom had borrowed was a mare that had given birth to her foal a few weeks earlier. Before taking her back into the barn Mom quickly milked the mare and held the cup so I could drink that milk.

Later that summer the fields looked exactly like I had seen them earlier that winter.

Some months later I woke up and everyone in the house came running over to see how I was doing! Everyone was so happy that I was awake. I was totally confused. I felt weak and washed up, my throat was hurting so intensely I could not speak. I tried to drink a glass of milk but it ran out of my nose as soon as I had swallowed it. My brothers were asking me to keep drinking more milk and kept on laughing because they had never seen anything like that before. They thought it was funny! I thought it was funny! Why was everyone so happy now while I was in such terrible pain?

Much later I found out that I had come out of my coma. When I told Mom about those experiences many years later she was totally perplexed. I was unconscious to the world but

I observed and was aware of a lot of things that were going on around me. Three-hundred-sixty degrees around me. My wakefulness did not last too long. I felt very weak and slept a lot. The first time I was allowed to go outside by myself to play the apples on the trees were the diameter of a dime.

Being able to play outside again was wonderful and shortly after I found a railroad freight car lying in the ditch across the street. It was made of wood, had four wheels and sliding doors on one side. It was about a foot long. I loved it. I cleaned it up and tied a string to it so I could pull it around wherever I went. I was now the proud owner of a toy. I found myself pulling it around everywhere I went and if I found myself passing a field of potatoes I would dig up a few potatoes and put them into my wagon. I would look around for vegetable fields and gardens. One tomato here, a few carrots there, green beans, cucumbers and whatever I could find. There were people around working in the fields and gardens but no one was paying attention to me.

When my wagon was full I would turn around and take it home and hand the wagon over to my Mom. She just looked at me and took it from me, emptied it, cleaned it and gave it back to me. She did not ask where I had found the wagon or the vegetables and I did not feel the need to explain it.

I have no idea what we lived on for that one year but I don't remember ever being hungry.

Many years later I told Mom about the neighbor who came over with the bowl of soup for me and the conversation the two of them had beside my bed. Mom was totally astonished that I was able to observe and remember all of that, after all, I had been unconscious and unresponsive to every contact.

We moved to the West

My mother volunteered to work for the Russians as an interpreter and about one year after the war had ended they told her that she would be allowed to move to West Germany if she could prove that the head of the household, my father, lived in the West. My mother had received a postcard from my father shortly after he got drafted. It was mailed from France. He explained that he was captured by the French and was held there as a prisoner of war. She showed it to them and received a pass to leave East Germany to move to the West legally. During this past year many Germans tried to escape to the West and were shot dead whenever they were caught trying to cross the border.

The day we boarded the train to leave East Germany was quite exciting for me. Everybody threw their belongings, bags and bundles of clothing and packages and boxes of personal valuables into the corner of the wagon until it almost reached the ceiling. My mother told me to crawl up to the top of the goods and just sit up there until we arrived at our destination. It would keep me safe and I would not get trampled up there. I loved it up there! I pretended to be a princess and all the people below me were my subjects. The train we were in was a freight train with sliding doors on one side. (When I saw the movie 'Dr. Zhivago' all I could think of was: 'right on – been there – done that!') The inside was one huge room now stuffed with people standing side by side holding on to each other and on to small children and whatever valuables they were trying to protect.

After some time the train stopped and a lot of commotion was going on outside. The sliding doors were ripped open and Russian soldiers armed with guns entered and were shouting to see the boarding passes. My mother had her boarding passes in her hand and was pushed over to one side and allowed to stay as were others who were able to show their boarding passes. People who did not have a pass handy were pulled off the train and fell to the ground outside as they were pushed out. This took a short few minutes and the soldiers stepped off the wagon and slid the doors shut behind them. There seemed to be a lot of people outside all screaming and crying horrendously and fighting to get back on to the train. We heard a lot of gun shots and the screaming and crying stopped. The people that were pushed off the train had all been shot to death. The train was ordered to continue on its way. We had just crossed the Russian border and were now in West Germany.

Bad Segeberg Refugee Camp

We arrived in Bad Segeberg. They had set up a refugee camp some time back. We stayed there for a few days until they found a place they could send us to. From all the experiences we have had until then this definitely was the worst of them all. We were directed to settle down in a large, gym-type room. There were no walls or divisions anywhere. No beds anywhere in sight. People slept on the floor on blankets. The floor on the outside edges was inhabited first and the people who arrived later took their places further into the middle of the floor. The very center of the floor was still empty. I will never forget our neighbors. A frail elderly couple was lying on a blanket beside us holding hands. They did not speak to each other or to anyone around them. They just lay there holding hands and looking up to the ceiling.

The first morning after waking up I had to go to the bathroom and went outside to find an outhouse. A lot of people were out there trying to pass time. Some were just standing around while others were chatting with each other and a lot of them were lined up at one of the four outhouses.

I really had to go. I could not understand why they all lined up at that one outhouse when there were three others there just waiting to be used. It had rained over night and it was still drizzling so the ground was wet and slippery. The outhouses all looked the same. They were eight or ten units side by side built out of raw plywood mounted on a dug out hole in the ground. The hole was a couple of feet wider than the outhouse and the outhouse I had chosen was missing the board that let people step into and out of the opening at the end of the wall. That did not seem to be a problem for me and I jumped across the gap and went in to do what I came to do.

I was quite shocked that there were no partitions between the holes. Everyone would have to sit down on the toilet side by side without any privacy. I was quite proud of myself that I had chosen this outhouse. I was all by myself and had all the privacy I could wish for. Privacy yes – toilet paper no.

So far - so good. As I stood in the doorway ready to get back out I understood why no one had chosen this outhouse. I stood there for quite a while trying to figure out what to do. I had to jump out. I could see that if I did not make it I would fall into the hole filled up to the brim with stenching fecal matter.

There were several people standing around not too far from me but no one was paying attention to me and my quest and even though some people were looking at me no one offered to help me. I jumped the hardest jump I ever had to make reaching the other side and started to wobble. The ground was wet and slippery and I threw myself forward to make sure I would not fall backwards and slide into the hole.

Our new Home

Our new home was to be Gudow, a large village in northern Germany. A farmer had an empty room in the attic with two beds which he had to let us use. The room was very narrow. The beds were standing against the wall end to end with a narrow walk between them and the wall. There was an empty space behind the door at the foot end of one of the beds where we piled up all our belongings. My mother slept in one bed with my two sisters and I was to sleep in the other bed with my two brothers.

The beds were quite narrow so I decided to sleep at the foot end. This did not work out that well because I was being kicked again and again every time my brothers moved. Distraught by this I took an armful of straw out of my bed and put it down on the floor beside the bed and slept on that instead. I used my pillow to cover myself. It was peaceful and seemed all right until I felt mice running across my face and body. I did not mind the mice but I was getting upset because they did not let me sleep.

Night after night they would pester me and one day as I was sitting on the floor polishing my shoes one of the mice was checking me out. I felt I should teach it a lesson and caught it. I took it by the tail and carried it downstairs to the back of the farmyard and immersed it into a puddle of water while telling it not to wake me up every night. This went well for about three or four dips until it stopped moving. I had no intentions of killing that poor mouse and felt awful for taking its life. The mouse had never hurt me and killing it because it had annoyed me seemed awfully mean. I will never get over it.....

Some time went by and my mother managed to get permission to move to the main floor in the same farmhouse. We now had a regular room with an adjoining bedroom. The room was heated with a wood burning ceramic tile heater which had a round lid on top to refill it with firing wood whenever it had burned down. Mom cooked on top of that heater. I remember the best potato pancakes she had ever made. She grated the potatoes and an onion and squeezed out all the water, added some salt and formed patties which she baked on top of that lid.

Shortly before Mom died I had made potato pancakes for lunch and mentioned to my Mom how I missed the pancakes she had made way back then. They were the best ever! What was her secret? She looked really puzzled and asked me a few times if I really meant that? She told me she was devastated because that was all she had to feed us that day. No butter to fry them in, no eggs to add to the batter and no flour to hold the batter together. Just potatoes and an onion! We ate them plain – no sour cream to top them off with. I was so pleased I had mentioned those pancakes to my Mom. Later on I realized just how much she had really needed to hear that.

We had no processed foods in those days and every meal Mom prepared was made from scratch. Groceries were hard to come by and a lot of times we would buy whatever was available. One day Mom had come home with packaged soup. That was a first for her. After cooking it according to directions she stood behind us and watched our faces as we started to eat. No one said a word but our faces must have given us away. Mom apologized and told us we did not have to finish the soup – she could not stand it herself and did not expect us to eat it if we did not want to. That soup must have been quite horrid; this was the first time we were given that choice. No one said a single word and we all finished eating every single spoon full. The soup was made out of roots, weeds and herbs. Mom never served it to us again.

This was definitely a hard time to make it through the day buy I am having a hard time imagining what my mother felt emotionally. We knew we would never be able to go back home again and we all depended on Mom to keep us safe and alive through whatever happened. Not a small task for her! Whenever we seemed a little low in spirits Mom would tell us quite enthusiastically:

"We are not POOR!"

"We are NOT POOR!"

We heard her tell us that soo many times and we knew she meant it. I grew up knowing that I was not poor – no matter what – I would never be poor. To this day I give thanks for all the riches I experience daily.

Lammy

The years went on and things got better. Mom and my brother built a small barn down the raveen from our house. It had a large enough pig pen for three pigs, quite a large chicken coup above it, an area where our flock of geese slept and enough space to keep our firing wood dry and, of course, room for our Lammy. Lammy was our pride and joy. We would walk her down to the lake every day and put a pick into the ground so she had lots of grass to feed on until we brought her home in the evening. She was just like one of us kids. Whenever we would play hide and seek she would play with us. She would hide and wait until she was found and always amused us by how happily she jumped around because she was found. She would take turns standing behind the tree until we counted to ten and told her we were ready for her to come and find us. We would always pretend she had not found us but she would not give up. She would bump us with her head and push us until we fell over and started to laugh, at which point she would jump around like the happiest little kid before she would go on and look for the next one of us. She always knew how many children were playing and she never gave up until she had found every single one of us.

Mom told us about the encounters she had with her. She would be splitting wood in the barn and Lammy would tap on the trough in front of her to get Mom's attention. Mom would look up to see what she wanted but only noticed that she looked at Mom then looked up to the shelves under the ceiling behind Mom and then looked into her trough. She did this again and again because Mom did not understand what she was trying to tell her. After a while Mom followed her look and noticed she was looking at a sack of grains on that upper shelf that Mom would give her now and then for a treat. Lammy was asking Mom for a treat and she knew where the treat was being kept. We loved her! All spring, summer and fall we would go out and pick grass and weeds for Lammy and the pigs. In the fall we would collect chestnuts and acorns to feed them during the winter.

Lammy loved to have her wool shorn off every spring. She would jump around and dance like a little wild person for days. After we all went to bed in the wintertime Mom would sit beside her spinning wheel and spin the most beautiful yarn out of that wool. We knitted all our socks, mittens, caps, scarfs and sweaters – whatever we wanted and needed.

We worked hard every day to collect berries, fruit, mushrooms and firing wood. Collecting wood was the scariest for me. Mom would borrow a wagon from the farmers and we would go all around the other side of the lake because close to home the woods were picked clean. We were not allowed to break branches off the trees and could only pick up wood lying on the ground. It took a lot of running around to fill up the wagon.

This one evening it was beginning to get dark and I could hear the wild pigs rummaging around very close to us. I was afraid of wild pigs because they were dangerous if confronted. I pleaded with my Mom to turn around and get home before anything happened. She told me we were fine and would not give up until the wagon was loaded to the top. It was dark by the time we started heading home. The wagon was hard to pull and not seeing where we were going did not help any. I was so stressed and thankful when we finally arrived home. I did not like collecting wood and we had to do it quite often.

Some memories just did not fit in

And then there were the other memories. I was about five years old. The memories were happy and very detailed but did not fit into anything I knew. A few weeks before my Mom died we were chatting about the good old days and I brought up some of those memories again. I just wanted to know how old I was at that time. My Mom did not know what I was talking about. I gave her more details. I described the kitchen and living room and mentioned that I could not remember the back wall. There seemed to be no back wall. I only remembered that it was all black back there. The floor was made of black earth and whenever Mom was sweeping it I would take a handful of moist white sand out of the pail on the floor and jump up and down asking excitedly:

"Now Mama, now? Can I do it now?"

I felt that moist sand in my palm and was so excited because Mom let me sprinkle the sand on the freshly swept floor to make it look pretty.

"Yes, I remember that - but that was not you! That was Wilhelmine."

"Wilhelmine loved to sprinkle the sand on the floor. She used to hop and dance around until I said: "Yes, now.""

"You were not even born yet!""

"No Mom that was me, that was me. I loved to sprinkle the sand on the floor! I was doing it every time you swept the floor."

"I remember how the sand felt in my hand."

"That was me….."

"How could you know about that?"

"Who told you?"

"Did Wally tell you?"

We both got a little excited and upset and Mom stopped talking – she just turned white and stared at me – after a long while I heard her say:

"Oh my God, you are Wilhelmine!"

Needless to say at this point I also turned white and stopped talking. After a few quiet moments Mom told me that Wally, my oldest brother was just a newly born baby. He could not have told me and there was no one else around, just Mom, me and my baby brother.

Our house had burned down and we lived in the front of the barn until the new house was built. The reason I did not remember the back wall was because there was no wall. It looked black back there because there were no lights in the barn.

Mom and I did not talk about this for the next few days. We both needed time to digest our new discoveries. Mom had been seriously ill for over a year and shortly after our chat she had to be taken to hospital. At this time I found out that Mom was not expected to live more than a week or two. She died one week later. I am sorry we never talked about that again, but I am grateful I found out as much as I did. It started an unbelievingly long and interesting path which explained my whole present life for me.

Wilhelmine was Mom's first Baby. She lived to be five years old and had died of diphtheria and scarlet fever. Mom talked about her often and told us she had planned to grow old with her and never stopped missing her. I definitely understood that Mom had not gotten over losing her baby girl but every time she talked about her death I became very sad and silently said:

"Hmmm, I am here....."

I really did not understand just what that meant. In my heart there was only one me. I was born again about five years after Wilhelmine had died.

Did I come back to grant Mom that wish? A few months after Mom got sick I asked her to move in with me so I could look after her. I had two little girls to raise and could not drive down to see her every day. She was happy to do that but at that time we were both in the dark about what we had discovered a few months later.

First Steps

About two years after Mom had died I was sitting in my living room late at night sewing something when I heard Mom call out behind me in a loud, urgent, frustrated tone of voice:

"Martha!"

My head flipped back to where the voice was coming from and I answered:

"Yes!"

I expected to see my Mom there but instead I was looking at the wall – a blank wall – no Mom! It really threw me. I was alone in the house with my two young daughters sleeping in the bedroom behind that wall. I could not think straight and sat there for quite a long time. I did not try to communicate with Mom and after getting too sleepy to stay up any longer I decided to go to sleep. I felt safe. I knew my mother would never hurt me.

The next morning I got up, dressed my girls and had breakfast with them before I took them to my best friend and neighbor to see if she could look after them for a few hours. I just had to go to the main library in downtown Calgary. Had no idea why, I just had to. I had never been to that Library before so when I arrived I just walked over to the elevator and pressed the button to go to the highest floor. As I stood there I looked around and decided to turn left and go see what I would find in that corner. To my surprise I found myself in the parapsychology section. Without too much effort I looked at a lot of those titles and picked five or six books to take home. As I read each book I could have sworn my Mom was talking to me, telling me what living and dying is all about. What I learned was totally fascinating and I was not sure I could accept it all. The more I read the more confused I became and question after question popped into my head.

A few months later I was sitting on the bus going home when the bus stopped in front of a drugstore to pick up new passengers. Lost in thought I was looking into the drugstore window and noticed a carousel displaying paperback books. Even though I was unable to read the titles one of the books really attracted my attention. I had to have it! Before the doors closed I jumped out of the bus, ran in to the drugstore and bought the book. When I came back out the bus had left and I had to wait for the next one, buy a new ticket and get on home.

Once I started reading that book my annoyance was replaced with awe! It seemed all the questions that popped up while reading the first set of books were answered by this one!

I *stopped fighting*

By this time my frame of mind had changed enough that I wanted to stop fighting and learn more and more about all the occurrences I could not understand. I wanted to know what my life was all about. I wanted to know why I remembered Wilhelmine's childhood. Before I fell asleep I asked to be shown, in dreams, in a clear and simple way, anything from previous lifetimes that is of importance to me in this lifetime. Since all of this was new to me I had no expectations. Every night I repeated my request. A few months went by and one morning I woke up with a start. The dream I had was extremely realistic and physical. I stood on a beige cobblestone street between two tall men in dark robes. It felt like I was about ten years old. Even though no one introduced us I knew one of them was Friedrich Schiller and the other one was Johann Wolfgang von Goethe. My two favorite German Poets. One of them put his arm around my shoulders and with a light squeeze told me:

"Yes, you are/were his daughter!"

Then the other one put his arm around my shoulder and while looking straight into my eyes kindly said:

"Yes, you are/were my daughter!"

The words are/were were one word. No lips moved as these sentences were spoken but I heard them loud and clear:

I was Goethe's daughter, oh my God, I was Goethe's daughter.

During the next few weeks I researched everything I could find about Goethe without success. After a while I dropped it. I had moved and needed to find a new doctor for my daughter who had developed a serious case of tonsillitis. My new neighbor offered his help by giving me his doctor's name and assured me he was the best person to see. As we entered the clinic the receptionist told us that doctor was on vacation but we could see the one taking his place. We sat in the office waiting for the doctor to arrive. As the door opened our eyes met and locked. The doctor walked over to his desk, stood there for quite a long while, said:

"Excuse me"

and walked out again. Our eyes never broke contact. I felt extremely perturbed. Did not know what had just happened. Kept asking myself what the problem was and knew I had to hang in there and handle it. After the longest time the door opened again and the doctor walked over to his desk with his eyes glued to the floor. O.K. I took a deep breath and was assured it was not just me. After we left the clinic I could barely cope. I was an emotional mess. Feelings I never felt before were overwhelming me. I could not even put my finger on what I was feeling besides hate, love, fear, admiration, loneliness, happiness, confusion. Definitely confusion. I was floating on air. My feet did not touch ground for at least three days. Not only did this happen every time I had to see him but between late afternoon, when I phoned to make an appointment until the next morning I would lose between eight to ten pounds.....

Another step

A few years went by. I went back to school and met some interesting new friends. One of the ladies, Irene, was interested in parapsychology, astrology and reincarnation. We had so much to talk about. One evening she called me to see if I could see a German friend of hers who was not feeling well. Irene asked me if I could take her to see my family doctor but after talking with her for a while we decided she should just see her own family physician since he was already familiar with her. Later that week there was a huge Psychic Fair happening at the Calgary Stampede Grounds. The three of us decided to go and check it out. On the way over there Irene's friend was telling us something about her hometown, Vienna. I got very excited and gave her a big hug and said:

"Maybe that is where I know you from."

Right after I had said that I wondered what my problem was – I had never been in Vienna and I was not in the habit of hugging people I did not know that well. Once inside we signed up for a free psychic reading that was being offered by a famous psychic. I was the first one to go in. The psychic was in a semi trance and asked if there was anything in particular I wanted to know about. I asked him if I was Goethe's daughter in a previous lifetime. He went through Goethe's life and ended up telling me that he had four sons, three stillborn and one lived with mental disabilities. Well, so much for that dream. My next question was about my new family doctor. Have we known each other in previous lifetimes? After a few moments he excitedly burst out:

"Yes, yes, there it is, there it is!"

"Not Goethe, not Goethe, you were Schiller's daughter!"

Schiller was a physician but spent every free moment writing poetry and often expressed his frustration in his poems and plays. The early 1780's were the beginning of his agonizing pile-up of debts. He moved around a lot to get away from his creditors. Even though he was in a relationship and deeply in love he had to drop everything again and run because he could not afford to be found. His girlfriend was pregnant at this time but he did not know that. She married an older farmer and they raised the child together.

That child was me.

I had a wonderful life but I had never forgiven my father for breaking his contract with me. Schiller was my chosen parent, my mother, his girlfriend, was his partner. Here he had left me before I was even born and I was totally dependent on being raised by the parent who was not my first choice. In my heart I had never forgiven him for that! When my reading was done Irene's friend went in and when she came out she was laughing hysterically.

"Would you believe what he told me?"

"He told me I had an illegitimate child with Schiller."

"What garbage!"

Well, I kept my reading to myself. A few weeks later she had left her husband and moved in with an older man that we all knew. This person knew my family doctor personally and one Sunday afternoon they were invited to come over and spend the day together. I had mentioned my doctor's name the first evening we met and when she saw that name on the doorbell she almost fainted. Once they entered the doctor introduced his new fiancée to them. Low and behold, they booth looked like they could have been identical twins. I have no idea how the afternoon went but shortly after that she left Calgary and no one knew what had happened. My doctor married his fiancée and after two children the marriage broke up. My question is: did he marry the wrong woman? Seems to me he should have made it up to his old girlfriend and married her.

I felt privileged to have soo much information about all of us and wanted nothing more than to sit down to have a good heart-to-heart talk about it. Just the three of us! How many people would ever have an opportunity such as this? My doctor knew he was the reincarnation of Schiller but started to shake and become extremely edgy whenever we got into that conversation. Regretfully I stopped bringing it up. He was not ready to deal with this part of our past and even though it was painful it was important for me not to pursue it.

Free Will

Years later I learned about free will. Schiller and I had a contract to spend that life time together as father and daughter. Having free will he had every right to make decisions that changed that outcome but I was unable to accept that and was unable to forgive him for leaving me stranded. In order to understand free will completely I was born into this lifetime to experience how a mother feels raising a child that does not understand and appreciate the effort and loving care a mother is capable of giving. I am experiencing what it feels like not to be the chosen parent. I am also learning to appreciate how it feels to be loved completely by a child as the chosen parent and I learned how to quiet a shattered heart when I found myself helpless in a totally hopeless situation.

Free will brings with it unimagined responsibility to all involved. If we don't understand it and force others to do our will, whether by manipulation or control, we will come back again and again until we get it. Time is of no essence. If we get it this time around we move on to the next experience, if we don't get it there is another life time and another and another. We are here for a very long time.....

Soft Voice

Quite a few people comment on my voice. I know it is not very loud but I never gave it any thought until a new acquaintance asked me if I had diphtheria as a child. Hearing that was a surprise. How would he know that? He told me he had the same problem with his own voice. The diphtheria damaged his vocal cords and now he needed a lot of air to make them work. A lot of times he is unable to finish his sentence and has to take a quick breath so he can finish speaking. Well, I am experiencing that myself but did not know it was the result of having been sick.

I started grade one in three different countries. Shortly after the war had ended and a lot of our male teachers had died fighting the war they filled the gap by allowing students to teach until they got married. Our first grade teacher at this time was one of those student teachers. She was very pleasant but had no clue how to keep the students disciplined. I was standing up answering whatever I had been asked but the teacher could not hear me because the kids were making a racket. She kept asking me again and again to speak up and after a while most of the kids were shouting right along with her:

"Louder" "Louder"

My voice did not get any louder so she asked me to go outside the door and shout through the key hole. I really thought that was stupid so I closed the door behind me, leaned against the wall opposite that door and just stood there listening to the students scream at me that they still could not hear me and I needed to shout a lot louder.....
After a seemingly long time the teacher opened the door and saw me there leaning against that wall. Perplexed she told me to go sit down at my desk. I was never again asked to shout. I was seven years old. When I think about that now I am quite impressed with myself. I was definitely born with that personality and free will was important to me even then.

The next three years were very pleasant. Since the teacher could not handle the class she read us a lot of stories to keep us quiet. I think we heard every story that had ever been written. A few years later a new principal came to our school and after testing everyone's progress we found out that our class failed in everything and he did not care how many stories we were familiar with! Wow! That was bad news for us. He took over as our main teacher and gave us about four hours of homework every day to catch up with our studies. Double that on Saturdays. Of course we revolted. We never got any homework on Saturdays! Oh yeah! Well he doubled up on that again, after all, we had all day Sunday to do it! There was no way we could win.

One evening I was playing with the girl across the street, and when she had to go inside to do her homework I went in with her and watched. She was a few years older than me and I looked up to her. As she was writing her sentences my eyes just popped. She had the most beautiful handwriting I had ever seen. She drew every letter so carefully her page looked like a piece of art. I could hardly wait to do my homework that way. I ran home and looked at my work. I must have missed penmanship classes. My handwriting looked scribbled and the pages looked like the chickens had been scratching around in there to find some worms or something. Well, I wrote every letter slowly and carefully just like she had done. Finally I was done and extremely proud of myself! The next morning we had to put our work on the edge of our desk and the teacher would walk around to check it and initial the page. When he looked at my work he angrily asked:

"Who did your homework?" "Who wrote this?"

"I did my own homework." "I wrote this myself!"

After being yelled at and told not to lie to him he finally told me to go to the blackboard and prove to him that I could write like that. Of course I could write like that! He stopped yelling at me, picked up my workbook and held it up for everyone to see. He walked up and down the classroom to show it to everyone and praised me over and over again. When he was finished with our class he crossed the hallway and showed it to those students. They were three years older and my brother was one of them. I felt like I was ten feet tall. I had not received attention like that since I was one year old and showed my siblings that

I had grasped the concept of communication. The praise went on for a few more days and then everything went back to normal.

Now what?

I had really enjoyed all that praise and attention and did not want it to come to an end. In the weeks that followed I tried very hard to come up with noteworthy ideas and when the next report card came out I was rewarded for trying so hard. Up to then I passed every grade, not with flying colors but I passed. That was all that was required but this time I did pass with flying colors. All my marks were 'excellent' and 'very good' compared to the old report cards that were marked 'satisfactory' or 'poor.' I kept it up and until I graduated I was the top-of-the-class student.

My voice never got any stronger and a few years after my grade one experience I surprised myself, actually I should say I shocked myself with my voice. Whenever I need a good laugh I think about this incident. It was extremely funny and a bit scary. It was a summer evening. It was already dark outside. I had come home and found the door locked so I sat down on the steps to wait for someone to come home and let me in. As I was sitting there floating around in that private little world of mine two large farm dogs came chasing down the walkway in front of me. They were in the middle of a fight and made a lot of hostile fighting and barking sounds. It really startled me because I heard myself letting out a bloodcurdling scream that scared even me! The two dogs tried to stop running but had so much force behind them that they slid down the walk for a couple of meters and crashed into the mesh wire fence at the end of the walk trying to get away from me. There was no way out so they had to turn around and run past me again to get away. I had never thought of a farmer's watch dog being afraid of anything but these two dogs forgot about their own fight and dashed past me to save their own skin.

That was power – my quiet soft voice was that powerful!

My Search began

I grew up in a religious family. Every night before I went to sleep I would kneel beside my bed and say my prayers. On Sundays we would go to church. Every Sunday the pastor told us we were sinners. We were born in sin. Unless we lived the life God wanted us to live we would die in sin and go to hell. That really bothered me. I was a very obedient child and tried not to hurt anyone and do whatever my mother told me to do. I did not understand what I was doing wrong. After coming home from church one Sunday I paid special attention to everything I did that week. I did not throw out or waste any food. I did all my chores. I did all my school homework as always. I did not talk back to anyone. I did not fight. I did not..... I did not..... I did not..... I passed with flying colors! The next Sunday at church I expected the pastor to mention that but instead I heard him angrily shout:

"You are all sinners!"

"You were born in sin and you will die in sin!"

That did it for me! Something inside me shut off and I knew this kind of religion had nothing to do with the God we believed in. At this point I think I was about twelve years old. I kept on going to church every Sunday but did not tell anyone about my change of faith. Once I turned fourteen I had to go to confirmation classes once a week. The pastor was our teacher and taught us much more than the catechism. Several times during that year he would lose his temper and start cussing and cursing in front of the class and a few times he would pick up his chair and come running towards us with the intention of beating up on us. We always beat him to it – before he had a chance to hit anyone we all dashed out of the classroom and waited around in the yard and eventually just went home.

Confirmation was a big day. Mom bought me a new black taffeta dress and a new coat. I got my first pair of dressy new shoes and for the first time I wore a pair of nylons. I was fifteen years old and all grown up! Before we left for church I went across the street to pick up a bunch of greens my neighbors had promised me for my scented Violets confirmation bouquet. On my way back our rooster came running across the street and flew up into the air to attack me. He did not recognize me. I was taken off guard but had to protect myself so I could go on to my confirmation. I kicked him with my foot and by chance hit him directly under his breastbone. He flew high into the air and landed on the cobblestone street like a pancake and did not move. I was heartbroken. He was our watchdog. He would not let anyone come to our door, not even the mailman. As I walked over to pick him up he pulled himself together and ran away like lightening. After that he always ran like crazy every time he saw me.

The confirmation service was being performed beautifully. Close to the end of it we were kneeling by the altar to receive our blessings. As the pastor was standing in front of me with his hands folded over my head giving me my blessings all I could think of was:

"Please dear God – don't let him have a fit now!"

We came to Canada

One day in 1954 Mom came home and asked us:

"Who wants to go to America?"

We all looked at each other and started jumping up and down and cheered:

"I do!" "I do!"

The next day Mom walked to town and applied at the US Government Immigration Office to fill out the papers for immigration. She found out that we did not qualify but they told her to try the Canadian Immigration office. She came home with the sad news and asked:

"Who wants to go to Canada?"

Again we were jumping up and down and letting her know that we all wanted to go to Canada! The next day Mom walked back to town and applied for immigration to Canada. She had to sign a two-year contract for us to work in the sugar beets.

A few months later we went to Bremen for three days for the physical examinations. There was a lot of waiting around for our turns to get examined. The last examination we went through I will never forget. A huge meeting room had several tables set up close to the door with five or six men and several women sitting behind them looking out onto the floor. Both sides of the room had blankets strung up to make little changing rooms for the people taking part. The little rooms were about one and a half meters square. They put me and my younger sister and my Mom into one changing room. We could barely move. We were asked to strip down naked and wait for our name to be called. My mother was very embarrassed to be standing in front of us stark naked. No matter how cramped our living conditions had been in the past, we always respected each other's privacy. When my name was called I went outside and was told to walk to the middle of the room and stand in front of the row of tables. I was stark naked, O.K.? I had just turned sixteen! All the people waiting in those little changing rooms could see me. All the men and women were looking me up and down and after forever told me to turn around. I had to lift my arms a few times and after what seemed to be an extremely long time I was told to go back and get dressed. I don't remember any white doctors' uniforms and to this day I have no idea what this examination was for.....

None of us ever talked about it!

We came over on the M.S.Beaverbrae. It had been a freighter converted to transport immigrants from Germany to Canada. It took us eleven days until we arrived in Quebec City. From there we rode the train and arrived in Lethbridge three days later. The first morning I woke up in our new home I went into our living room and found my two brothers and my mother each standing quietly in front of a window and after a while they all changed position and walked to another window. After changing windows again my mother turned around and said in a most defeated voice:

"Oh my God – we are in Siberia!"

When we left Germany two weeks earlier the trees were green and spring flowers were in full bloom. Here in Canada it was terribly cold, the snow was at least a foot deep and absolutely everywhere. The land was so flat. We could see for miles and miles and saw nothing but snow and a few trees and shrubs here and there. It was the 29th day of April 1954.

Sugar Beets

The snow melted eventually and the beets were beginning to grow. Our work was waiting for us. We got up as soon as the sun rose and were on the fields until it was too dark to see. In the summer months that was from five in the morning until ten thirty at night. Mom would come out to the fields around nine every morning and bring us sandwiches and coffee. We would take a break and eat and get back to work until noon. After lunch we would work until five or six when Mom brought us something to eat and then back to work until it was too dark to see. I was always exhausted. When I went to bed after eating supper I would fall asleep while undressing. Mom would finish undressing me and put me to bed most evenings. As soon as I had fallen asleep Mom would be trying to wake me up. I was so sleepy every morning I never felt like I had slept at all.

We worked six days each week. Sunday was our day off. We would walk eight miles each way to attend German church most Sundays. Not that we missed going to church that much but it gave us an opportunity to meet and communicate with other German people who had come to Canada to find a better life.

The heat was another thing to get used to. I remember one day in particular. All summer long the heat was unbearable and often the temperature rose to one hundred and ten degrees. We hardly ever saw any clouds in the sky except this day. The cloud was maybe two meters in diameter and hardly moving. No wind anywhere. I watched the cloud as it very slowly moved towards the sun. Silently I was praying that it would give us some shade for a few minutes. Many hours later it was right above us; it had missed the sun by a few inches.

Even though we wore large sunhats and loose, long skirts and long-sleeved blouses to cover our bodies from getting sun burned, the back of my hands were so exposed to the sun that they burned over and over again. They became so inflamed and infected, all I had to do is close my fist and pus would squish out of little holes all over the back of my hands. The pain was unbearable. This lasted all summer and healed over just before the harvest started.....

On exceptionally hot days the farmer and his sons would sit on their porch drinking beer and placing bets on which one of us would drop dead first.

Harvesting the beets was a totally different story. The weather had cooled off and we no longer needed to wear those big straw hats to keep our face and neck from burning. The beets were loosened in the ground; all we had to do was pull them out, smash them together to make the dirt fall off and throw them down on the ground in a fairly straight line. After that we would take our machete, which had a strong pick at the end of the blade, and hit each beet with it to pick it up. We would then take hold of the beet and chop off the greens and throw the beet back down. We did this all day long – one beet after another.

When I arrived at the end of the field my back was hurting so badly all I wanted to do was straighten up and ease my pain. To my surprise I could not stand up straight, it seemed like I was frozen in this bent-down position and trying to stand up was unceasingly painful. Since I could not manage to straighten up I gave up on that idea and just turned around and worked my way back to the starting point.

The first day of this harvest when Mom came by to bring us our sandwiches we were more than ready for the break. I whirled my machete as far away as I could manage but to my surprise it was still attached to my hand. I repeated throwing it away a few more times but could not manage to get rid of it. My fingers were cramped around the handle so tightly I had to twist them open one at a time and was left with a hand that looked and felt gnarled and crippled. This went on day after day until all sixty acres of beets were harvested.

Moved into Town

After the second year was done we moved to Lethbridge. Mom had found a lovely furnished house for a price we could afford. We were thrilled. A house all our own. The first morning we woke up we all stood there looking at each other with a big question mark on our faces!

"'How did you all sleep?"

"Sleep?"

No, none of us had gotten any sleep. The house was built across the street of a train station. All night long the trains would run back and forth and back and forth again and again and again. All night long the banging just would not stop! The next night was exactly the same as the first night and we could hardly stay awake during the day. The third night must have been the same but by now we were used to it and too tired to pay any attention to it. We all slept like babies from then on. No one ever mentioned the train station again.

My *first* Date

Important encounters
Are planned by the soul
Long before the bodies see each other!

Paulo Coelho

The first job I got in Lethbridge was as a waitress in a Chinese restaurant. It was a walk in a park. I worked a few hours during lunch time, got a few hours off and went back for a few more hours during supper time. I loved it. I became friends with a German waitress named Renate. Renate was engaged to an Italian young man who came in for coffee quite often and always picked her up when she got off work. He started to bring his friend with him who paid a little too much attention to me. He kept asking me to go out with him. I was eighteen years old by now but had never been out on a date before. I did not know this young man. He was tall, dark and handsome but I could not see myself being alone with him for a whole evening. He never gave up. He started telling me we were going to be married so I would have to start dating him sooner or later. Of course, I thought he was kidding. A few weeks went by and Renate started encouraging me to go out with him. He had become quite familiar to me and I finally accepted a date. I was nervous. He picked me up after my shift and told me we had to stop over at his house first. He lived about five blocks away from the restaurant. I sat down on the couch while he went into the kitchen. I could hear him using a can opener. As I looked around the room I noticed a small round mirror on the living room wall right in front of me. I could see what he was doing behind me in the kitchen! As I watched him he finished opening a can, put the can opener down and picked up a little bag with white powder in it. He put a teaspoon of that powder into the can and stirred it in for a moment. He then came into the living room and handed me a spoon and gave me the can of peaches. I was in shock. I told him:

"No thank you!"

He insisted I eat the peaches.

I insisted I did not want any peaches.

He kept insisting and after a while he lost his temper. He put the can of peaches down on the coffee table and turned around in a flash and grabbed my neck with both his hands. He pushed me down on the couch and glared at me with his face only a couple of inches above mine. He looked crazed..... I knew my life was in danger and without having time to think about it I remained very calm. He pushed both his thumbs up against my neck and looking at his thumbs while nudging them against my neck and looking back into my eyes he spewed the words into my face:

"Two more inches and you've had it!"

I looked straight back into his eyes and with a kind, steady voice I heard myself say:

"Go ahead and kill me."

"I can not marry you when I am dead, can I?"

As soon as I had said that he lifted his hands off my neck and sat up. He looked at his hands like he had never seen them before. His heavy breathing settled down and he seemed to return to normal again. We did not talk about this any more and he took me home.

He still came into the restaurant every day and acted like nothing had happened.

"Be careful with your words
Once they are said
They can only be forgiven
Not forgotten"

Unknown

I wanted to get away from all of this and moved to Ford McLeod and applied for work as a waitress in a newly opened Greek restaurant. The work was great. I loved working with the new staff and the only thing that bothered me was one of the waitresses. She did not like me and called me a 'dirty old stinking DP' every chance she got especially in front of customers. I did not let on that it bothered me for several months until one evening when we were cleaning up shortly before closing. I had a bowl with sudsy cleaning water and a fluffy cheesecloth in front of me and was washing the counter top. She was standing beside me and going on and on with her 'dirty old stinking DP' remarks. Without planning to do it I had lifted the cheesecloth out of the bowl and planted it directly on her face. With a firm twist and a big smile I heard myself saying:

"See, that's what a dirty old stinking DP does!"

The couple of steady customers sitting at the counter at that time broke out into a hearty laugh and winked at me while saluting me with a thumbs-up. She never called me that again. Actually, I don't remember that she ever talked to me after that.

Post=traumatic Stress

While still working at that restaurant I went to the movies with the girl I shared my room with. We saw a war movie. Soldiers, very young soldiers, were getting off a war ship and ran as quickly as they could into the woods to take their positions to defend that area. They looked scared. All I could think of was that most of them would never come home again. They would lose their life before they had an opportunity to live it. I broke out into a loud, hysterical crying spell. I was shocked. I could not stop the crying. I sobbed and sobbed out loud. I am sure everyone in the theater could hear me. My friend told me to cry all I wanted and not to worry about what anyone thought about it. I had a few moments when I calmed down but before the movie was finished I broke down several more times and cried uncontrollably without being able to stop it.

After the movie we wanted to go to a restaurant and have something to eat but I was uncomfortable with that idea. I was calm now but what if I broke out into another crying spell inside the restaurant? Well, we went inside and all was well. After we left the restaurant I broke into my crying routine one more time as we walked home.

The next day at work a young man who obviously had been at the movies the night before asked me, with a very caring tone of voice:

"Why did you cry at the movies last night?"

He was barely finished asking the question and I was in the middle of another terribly loud crying spell. I turned around and dashed out of the restaurant to try and calm down. For the next two weeks it happened a few more times but not as forcefully as the first day. What amazed me was that the only time I ever cried before was the day I got lost in my grandmothers garden twelve years earlier. I was also amazed that I had no control over any of it. I could not control the loudness, which was really embarrassing, and I could not control when I started to cry or when I was finished crying.

Many years later I borrowed the same movie so I could watch it again. To my surprise nothing happened throughout the whole movie. No tears – no howling! Whatever I had built up inside me was gone.....

I *stole my one and only* Photo

After a while we all moved to Calgary. I loved it there. I found a great job and made a lot of new friends. Mom had bought a house for us and having come to Canada was finally beginning to pay off. One day Mom brought out our family photo album and a bunch of loose photos and spread them out on the kitchen table. She told us to pick whichever photos were important to us and to divide them between us. Both my brothers and my sister were busy checking them out but I had my eye on only one photo. I did not want anyone to take it! I slowly reached across the table and put my hand over it and gently slid it towards me. No one had objected so I slid it below the table and just sat there holding my precious photo while everyone was picking and choosing and dividing the rest of them. Once everyone was finished with their selections I asked if they all were happy with their choices. I asked a second and third time and nobody wanted to make any changes. I took that as an O.K. and left the room with the only photo I wanted and hid it in my dresser drawer.

The photo I took was the only picture Mom had of Wilhelmine. She seems to be two or three years of age. Mom and Dad are sitting side by side. My father is holding Wilhelmine on his lap and my mother is holding my newly born brother, Waldemar, in her arms. I did not find out how important this photo was in my life until quite a few years later.

My *first* tea cup reading

Where I grew up we had a lot of gypsies moving through the village offering fortune telling of all kinds. I didn't know anyone who had any readings done but the whole thing intrigued me. I was employed at a bank and every coffee break we went next door to the coffee shop for coffee. Quite often I saw an older lady, all dressed in black, reading a tea cup for different people. I was told she was really good at it. I could not resist. I booked a reading but had no idea what to expect. I think I just had to try it.

The first thing she told me was that she saw two marriages in my cup. She turned the cup around and back and forth and finally explained that she could not make out what to make of it – anyway – the marriages would not work out.

The next thing she told me was that I would go on a little trip and would see and cross many bridges. That sounded a little friendlier and a few months later I received an invitation from a friend, who had moved to Saskatoon, to come and visit him and spend the holidays with him. I had never been to Saskatoon. My friend was driving me around town and showed me all his favorite places. He stopped the car on top of a bridge and with pride he told me to look all the way down the river. Wow, I was looking at bridge after bridge crossing the river uniting the two parts of the city. It was a beautiful sight and really took me off guard. This was what the tea-cup reader had told me about.

There were a few more things the tea-cup reader had told me but I did not remember the details. The one message I did remember was that I would get married late in life and would be very successful.

As time went on I had realized that she was right on with my two marriages that would not work out. I was engaged to be married to Jasmin's father and the wedding plans fell apart two months before the wedding was to take place. Two years later I was engaged to Teresa's father, who I thought was the most amazing man I could have ever met. That also fell apart. Now all I had to look forward to was a marriage late in life – late in life? How late is late?

I read the tea leaves
As if they were words left over
From a conversation between two cups.
Kenny Knight

My second tea cup reading

Many years later I studied with a religious group who really condemned all types of fortune telling. According to them this was tied up with the dark forces and was not to be taken lightly. I was not convinced. I heard of a tea-cup reader who was highly respected by the people I talked to. She seemed to be the best reader anyone had ever tried. I made an appointment. As I sat there drinking my tea I sincerely asked for guidance. I wanted to know the truth one way or another. My statement was: 'If she is backed by dark forces she will not be able to get through to me.' 'If she is working with light I give her permission to do my reading.' I was getting excited; it had been a long time since my first reading. She sat down, introduced herself and after some friendly chit-chat she picked up my cup and studied it. She turned it around a few times and after what seemed to be a long time she slammed my cup down on its saucer, angrily announced that she could see nothing there to tell me, pushed herself away from the table and stormed away!

I was perplexed – now what was that all about?

UFO *Sighting*

A few years after moving to Calgary I had just come home from a dance and sat in front of our house chatting with my date. The house was built on top of a hill and we could overlook the whole horizon reaching from the east all the way to the west. Suddenly I noticed a huge ball of light appear directly on the north of the horizon. It was orange in color and slightly vibrated back and forth as it moved at a steady pace eastward. It was quite bright but not blinding. The outside of the light was softly tapered, it did not look as smooth as the full moon. We watched the light move all the way across until it stopped exactly at the east point. It stood still for maybe a minute or two and started to move back across the horizon until it stopped at the north point where it had first appeared. After a minute or two it shot backwards and disappeared.

The newspapers did mention a strange sighting the next day but it did not create a lot of attention. A few years later while having a coffee I asked my date what he had thought of that sighting. To my surprise he did not remember seeing anything like that. I could not believe anyone could have forgotten such a unique experience. I had never forgotten it and often wondered where it had come from and why it had visited us.

Are we being watched?

I was a single parent and wanted to raise my daughters myself instead of taking them to a baby sitter so I worked from home translating legal documents from German into English. One afternoon my employer dropped by to deliver a new set of documents that needed to be translated and he noticed that my TV was not working. I explained that the picture tube had burned out and we had to do without TV until I could afford to replace it. I was doing bible studies at that time and my bible was lying on the coffee table. Laughing hysterically he pointed to the bible and said:

"Why don't you just pray and ask God to give you a new TV"

I was startled and answered calmly:

"When I pray I don't ask God for things, I thank God for what I have."

He really found that amusing because he could not stop laughing for quite a while. After he settled down he asked me:

"You thank God for what YOU have?"

"You THANK God for what you have?"

"Really"

The only answer I had was:

"Yes, every day"

"I thank God every day for what I have!"

Needless to say I was talking about my two little sweethearts and the overwhelming privilege of being allowed to be their Mother!

About a week later my doorbell rang. As I opened the door I saw my TV repairman standing there with a giant box telling me he came as soon as he could. He told me I had called him and told him I was ready for the new picture tube. We argued back and forth because I had not made that call and he swore it was me because he recognized my voice and I was the only person on his list who needed a picture tube. I explained to him I didn't have the money to pay for it yet, he had better take it back and we would try again in a few months.

He had a better idea. The Husky Tower had just been finished in Calgary and he was the person in charge of installing all the electricity. He offered to take me out to dinner to the tower with the revolving dining room. It was the newest and most beautiful dining place in Calgary. He wanted to show it off and treat me to a special evening. Of course I declined. Again and again I told him I could not do that until I could no longer look at his disappointed face and gave in.

"No strings attached?"

"No strings attached!"

"All I want you to have is an evening you will remember for a very long time!"

Well, he installed the picture tube and the next evening he took me out to the Tower for an amazingly wonderful dinner. The food was perfect. The waiters were very attentive and extremely funny. The electricity worked like a charm even though I didn't understand all the work that went into it. After dinner he took me home, unlocked my door for me, gave me a big hug and expressed what a great evening he had and thanked me for allowing him to take me out.

It is well to give when asked,
But it is better to give unasked,
Through understanding;
And to the open-handed
The search for one who shall receive
Is joy greater than giving.

Khalil Gibran

A few days later my employer dropped by to bring me some more documents that needed to be translated. I was so overjoyed by what had happened I turned on the TV and waving my hand squealed:

"Ta-daaaaa!"

"God heard us the other day and look what he gave me!"

This time, after I finished telling him the whole story, he did not laugh – actually he did not say a single word. I often think about the angel who made that phone call. I would love to meet her.….

We are not alone

The Evergreens from Toronto came to Calgary and I signed up to spend a whole Sunday with them. I was so excited. The feeder bus did not run on Sundays so I had to walk down to the main bus stop which was about fifteen blocks away. About fifty feet in front of me a man from my neighborhood was heading into the same direction. Half way down the street he was passing a house and slowed down to talk to a small dog that just came out of that yard. The dog seemed very happy about the attention he was getting. I could see his tail wiggling and was looking forward to coming closer to him but as soon as I approached the dog turned on me. His hair was standing straight up from the head all the way down to his tail. He growled viciously at me and blocked my way with an attack- mode stance which I did not want to experience. I had not expected this and was at a loss of what to do. I did not think a little ankle biter this size could do me much damage but if I had to turn around to go home to change my ripped nylons after cleaning myself up and applying a bunch of band aids, I would be late for the seminar. After standing there for a minute or so I had a brainstorm and silently screamed with every ounce of strength I could muster:

"I am not alone here!"

"Somebody – help me!"

Instantly the dog's stance changed – the hair flattened, the body went limp and the growling was replaced with whimpering. The dog turned around and waddled back into the yard.

I am still wondering what had happened there. Did someone try to stop me from experiencing what the Evergreens were teaching that day? Who was that someone? I really would like to know.

Cats are the Protectors
of our Souls

I believe cats to be spirits come to earth.
A cat, I am sure, could walk on a cloud
Without coming through.

Jules Verne

Around that time there have been other attacks that were similar that I was experiencing and am still unable to explain. I had rescued a beautiful white Persian cat from the SPCA. She usually slept at the foot end of my bed. Once in the middle of the night she woke me up with most frightening screams. As I sat up to see what was wrong I saw her sitting up in an attack position looking up to the ceiling above my head. She looked ferocious. Her fur was standing up all long her back and she was making barking sounds that I had never even heard from an attacking dog. The cat looked down at me a few times but did not stop what she was doing. I looked around but did not see anything. Needless to say I was too shook up to go back to sleep and after a while the cat calmed down and the two of us went downstairs for the rest of the night.

During the next few months there were several more attacks that were directed at my cat. I would be sitting on the couch with Catgut sitting on my lap and I would see a hand coming down from behind me grabbing the cat's head. The cat was asleep but would twist her head away from that hand but never quite made it. The hand always ripped some of the skin open before I managed to step in. The force seemed quite overwhelming. I could not figure out what the cat could have done to attract such attacks.

I believed that people always reincarnated as people because they were more highly evolved. Coming back as an animal would contradict that. I have changed my mind about that. I honestly believe that my mother had something to do with Catgut. Many times when I had to scold her she would just walk away from me, slowly sit down and turn around and give me that look. Every time it felt like my mother was looking back at me telling me what to do with that. The first few times I thought I was imagining it but after a while I gave in. Catgut died the same way my mother had died. That actually settled my uncertainty and I had a really hard time dealing with that. When these attacks were happening I wondered if they were meant for Catgut or for my mother.....

Electric treatment for my body

I had fallen asleep and woke up because of a tingling sensation all over my body. This was new. I had never experienced this before. I saw a mat about six inches above my body which was about four inches thick, twenty-four inches wide and over five feet in length covering my whole body from head to toe. It seems to have been constructed of very dense, silvery gray steam. Thousands of little bolts of lightning were shooting out of that little cloud and were hitting my body everywhere. It was getting quite intense and I seemed to be on the edge of tolerance. I knew I did not want to give in and held on for about five or ten minutes. It seemed to be a very long time. In the end I either lost consciousness or it just stopped. I could not make out how it ended. When I woke up I felt absolutely wonderful! I am still wondering what this treatment actually did for me.....

My first spiritual healing

A few years after coming to Canada I started studying every religion that intrigued me. Growing up I only knew two religions and here in Canada we had access to every religion I had ever heard of and then some. I studied several of them but was still looking. One Sunday my sister asked me to go to the Center for Positive Living with her. She had heard a lot of interesting details about the Center but did not want to go by herself. At the beginning of the service Dr. Aaftink told us to concentrate on someone in need of healing and proceeded with a healing meditation. I had never experienced a healing meditation and a little too flustered could not think of anyone who was not feeling well. Even though I had a slight fever, stuffed up head and terribly sore throat, I did not think it was proper to think of myself so I concentrated on my oldest brother. As a young fifteen-year old he had done so much to help my mother support all of us that I felt privileged to send him love and blessings to express my appreciation.

Around the middle of the meditation the left side of my face turned hot, slowly it spread towards my neck and the left side of my chest. Tears out of my left eye were running down my cheek and my nose was starting to run but only on the left side. After the meditation I cleaned up my face and asked my sister if I looked okay. I did not believe her when she told me it was fine so I asked my daughter. She also told me I looked fine. After the service the four of us went out for lunch and did not get home until late that afternoon. About five hours later my face and chest cooled off and my tears and nose stopped running.

When I woke up the next morning I was startled to notice how wonderful I felt! My temperature was normal, my head felt clear and my throat was no longer sore. I sat there for a long while trying to grasp the fact that the blessings I had sent to my brother had healed me. This was the first time I had taken part in a healing meditation and I, myself, experienced a healing.

This was where I belonged! There was no need for me to look any further. For the next ten years I hardly ever missed a service.

My life changed! I changed! The way I looked at things were totally new to me. I became a new being - I knew everything was possible – I knew I had found my teacher!

Be careful what you ask for

It was a beautiful summer afternoon. The service at the Center was finished and a group of single parents had planned to spend the rest of the day in the country. We found a deserted old farm near a pond and felt it was the perfect location for our picnic. The children all ran over to the barn to investigate and play. We heard a lot of screaming and shooting noises and laughed about how little effort it took to make the children happy. A few hours later we agreed to separate for a while so we could have private time for ourselves to pray, meditate or talk to the trees. I was not heavily into meditation but I loved the idea of talking to a tree. I found myself the biggest tree I could find, put my arms around it and said a few times:

"Somebody – talk to me – talk to me – talk to me….."

With my ear close to the tree I listened but could not hear a thing. I was a little giddy but proud of myself for trying.

After we got home and my daughters had gone to bed I was happy to stretch out and get some rest myself. Just as I was falling asleep I felt the mattress behind me dip and someone was lying down behind me. I felt a hand being placed on my hip and assumed it was my daughter, but something did not feel right….. she had not lifted my blanket to get into bed and if she lay down on top of the blanket it should have moved or pulled….. I lay there for a while trying to explain it to myself but too exhausted to move. Finally curiosity won and I turned my head to have a look.

To my astonishment there was no one sleeping behind me, my daughter was not there! I sat up and took a deep breath to calm myself down. After a while I quietly laid down again and felt that the person behind me was a woman, extremely lonely, desperately looking for human contact. I don't know how to explain it but I felt that she had been shot to death on that farm and was unable to move on because she did not realize she was no longer alive. When she saw me hugging the tree and heard me asking for somebody to talk to me she took me up on it. At this point I had a little chat with her and told her she was welcome to spend the night because I cared about her and we would talk some more in the morning. I did not feel afraid to go back to sleep and knew she would not hurt me. A thought ran through my head – did the children pick up on the shooting when they arrived at the barn?

The next morning I was downstairs in the kitchen making breakfast when my daughter came into the living room and dropped herself down onto the chair next to the kitchen and immediately jumped up from the chair and let out a shocking scream:

"Somebody is sitting on that chair Mom!"

She stood there pointing to the chair waiting for an explanation. I had not expected that and started to explain that we had picked up a woman at that farm and she had stayed over night with us. We spent some time talking about what we needed to do to help her move on and all three of us agreed to send her love and prayers to help her connect with her guides and explained to her that she had a better place to go to.

At lunch time my daughter came home from school, slowly walked into the living room, turned around a few times and announced:

"She is gone – there is nobody else here!"

Oh my aching back

Over the years my back started hurting more and more. It got so bad I could not stand by the sink and finish washing the dishes. After rushing through the first half of them I would run into the living room, stretch out on the carpet and wait for the pain to go away, then get back into the kitchen to finish washing the rest of them. For a few years I faithfully saw my chiropractor and got adjustments but they did not last very long. I was too young to be in such excruciating pain all the time.

One night just as I was falling asleep I noticed three men in light colored robes standing beside my bed. The two on the sides were quite tall and the one in the middle was very short, barely reached their hips. I was not startled. I knew they were my guides. Even though I had never seen them before I knew it was them. A psychic once described them to me and told me about our connection. I was quite giddy and giggled to myself that if I wanted to see them all I had to do was open my eyes. Actually I was seeing them very clearly with my eyes closed and I was too tired to open them so I just lay there watching them as they were peacefully observing me.

After a while the two tall men looked at each other and nodded a few times. Their lips did not move and I did not hear anything but I understood they were communicating with each other. After another nod the guide on the left side lifted his arms and put his hands on my back between my shoulder blades. When I noticed that his hands were sinking into my back right up to his wrists I screamed ... I screamed as loud as I could ... I was yelling to them to leave me alone ... to stop what they were doing ... I just screamed and screamed! The two tall guides looked at each other again and the one at the right nodded to the other one. I don't remember anything after that.

The next morning I was happily telling my daughters that my guides had fixed my back for me. They laughed and said:

"Good for you Mom! Good for you!"

Well, I had a lot of work that needed to get done so I went on with my day as soon as my daughters had left for school.

About six months later I was standing at the kitchen sink doing dishes again when a thought suddenly hit me:

'My back was not hurting!'

'My back was not hurting?'

'It was not hurting yesterday either!'

'It was not hurting the day before that and it was not hurting the day before that!'

I dried my hands and slowly walked into the living room and sat down. I was in such awe! My back had been so painful for such a long time and I did not take notice when it stopped hurting! I was at a loss and really did not know how to handle this. When I kept on screaming at my guides to stop what they were doing they put me out to shut me up so they could finish doing what they came to do in peace. It took me six months to remember! This happened about thirty-eight years ago and I have never had any back pain since then. Not even the slightest little whit of back pain…..

I love my guides! I tell them every day that I love and appreciate them!

While my body sleeps

Whenever I don't have a specific agenda that needs all my attention I ask my guides to take me to the Temple of Wisdom while my body sleeps. Sometimes I remember, but most of the time I do not. A lot of times I remember reading. I don't see the book I am reading from, all I see is a huge long line of print floating by in front of my face. I seem to be absorbing the content and at times I feel very impressed by it.

One night I felt I was frantically wiggling to get out of my body and finally I broke loose. I found myself floating high up in the sky above the clouds. Exhilarated, weightless and free. As I was looking down I could see my silver cord. It was attached to my stomach around the navel area and reached down many miles where I could see my body sleeping at the other end of it. The cord was not solid. It looked like it was made of steam. Soft, semi-transparent, silvery gray steam. Close to my stomach it seemed to be about twelve inches in diameter and as it softly drifted and curled towards my body it became narrower and narrower until it looked the size of a shoelace. My body also looked quite small at this distance.

As I was floating around I noticed quite a large opening in the clouds below me. The beams of light were shining through the opening adding a dreamy glow to the view. As I drifted through the clouds I saw it way down between all those buildings. It was impossible to miss. It was a huge cathedral made of pure gold. The Temple of Wisdom! Oh my God! The Temple of Wisdom! The light reflected so beautifully I had a hard time holding on to that … well, overwhelmed by all that excitement I woke up in my bed. I did not mind, at least this time I remembered seeing the temple from the outside.

Shooting through space

Another time I was shooting through space way out there - I have no idea where in this universe that may have been. My body consisted of a silvery grey metallic cone about five inches long. My conscience was totally in tact. I twirled around super fast and shot through space at an overwhelmingly high speed passing many different planets. I did not know where I was going and became a little afraid. I started to announce I no longer wanted to continue and wanted to go home. The cone did not slow down and I repeated my request again and again. At this point I was certain I no longer wanted to continue this and shouted with all my might that I needed to return – I had to go back home! Finally the cone slowed down little by little and the twirling also slowed down to a point where it almost stood still..... I woke up in my bed. I was soaking wet with perspiration and it took a while to get my heart beat back to normal.

I never wanted to do this again.

What is Time?

We are always told that time is something that only exists on earth and that past, present and future all exist at the same time. This may be simple for scientists to understand but I have always had a hard time imagining that. One morning I woke up quite startled and overwhelmed by what I had just experienced. Was it a dream? It really did not matter. Jesus explained the concept of time to me with a show and tell. He showed me our earth. It was huge and made of glass and had many, many layers all existing inside of each other. Each layer was rotating like our earth is rotating and Jesus pointed to one layer at a time talking about what was going on at that specific time. Then we came to the layer where Jesus was teaching. I could see him surrounded by his apostles and the crowds of people listening to him and following him wherever he went while at the same time he was standing beside me talking to me.

We spent a lot of time on that layer. I saw a lot of layers where I was a child and many layers that I did not recognize. I was so moved by that experience I could not get over it or maybe I should say I did not want to get over it. If I had to explain it I would say this was not a dream. It was real. Jesus explained the concept of time to me.

The Magic of Meditation

I was devastated! Totally devastated! Life was good and suddenly everything around me crashed. I had not done anything to cause this and as time went on I wondered if and how I could carry on. I made plans with a friend to go out for the evening to talk and to have a shoulder to lean on for a little while. As we arrived at the restaurant I noticed she had brought one of her friends along. Normally I would have loved that idea but this time I was bummed. I really did not want to talk about family matters in front of strangers and told my friend we would chat about my situation another time. Her friend kept asking questions and in a voice peculiarly rude she told me to read the book "The Four Agreements." I had no idea what she was talking about and really lacked the desire to find out! A little while later she put her fork down long enough to repeat her advice. I was really getting miffed. She hardly spoke to us and for the third time she told me I should read that book. I was glad the evening had come to an end and I could go home to feel sorry for myself in peace.

A few days later I had the television set on and switched to some talk show as someone was talking about how to meditate. I listened. The instructions were to sit in a comfortable position, hold our palms up and say:

'Dear God, my heart is open. Come live in my heart and ....'

Well, that sounded simple enough. I really wanted God to live in my heart and stated with every ounce of strength I could muster:

"Dear God, my heart is open. Come live in my heart and bring me joy!"

"Dear God, my heart is open. Come live in my heart and bring me joy!"

I kept repeating this request over and over again. I don't know how many times I said it, twenty times? Fifty? Seventy? I really don't know. I was so caught up with it that I had lost contact with time. Slowly I noticed that I was feeling a warm glow inside my chest mostly over the left side. That was my heart. Slowly I sat up straight and paid attention to what was happening. A little while later I felt the heat spread all across my chest all the way down to my waist and up to my neck. It felt like a big round ball of heat inside my body. It did not hurt in any way. It was very soothing and all the devastation and emotional pain I had felt for the last few weeks had disappeared. I was totally flooded with joy and all I could do was sit there and cry, cry, cry.....

Tears of joy!

Finally I stopped crying but the warmth and joy stayed with me every waking moment. Sometimes when I chatted with certain people the warmth went away. I would excuse myself as soon as I could and remove myself from that situation. A little while later the warmth would come back again and stay with me until I needed to make a better decision again. This lasted for about five years. As time went on the heat slowly cooled down and the ball grew smaller and at the end of the fifth year it was quite faint and in time I no longer felt it. I never lost the joy. It is still and hopefully always will be a part of me.

A month or so after that dinner date with my friend I found myself at Chapters Book Store. The clerk walked up to me and asked if she could help me. I remembered that Four Agreements book and asked her if they had one in store. The clerk spun around and with a little too much enthusiasm said:

"Oh wow, you have to read that book!"

Hello? What the heck is going on here! I grabbed the book, found myself a chair and started to thumb through it. I am not an impulsive shopper so I wanted to check it out. Not necessarily because I wanted to buy it but because I just needed to find out what this was all about! Well, after reading three pages I closed the book, got up and walked over to the cashier. I just had to take that book home.

Guess who had to read that book?

Right! I had to read that book! Apologies were definitely in order!

That book was written for me! Only once in my life have I read a book a second time. Once I have read a book I am pretty much finished with it. Except The Four Agreements! I can't believe I am actually admitting it. I have probably read it eight times already and I know I will reach for it again (and again).

The first book I ever read for a second time was 'Psychic Discoveries behind the Iron Curtain.' It was published in 1970. I read it in 1973. The authors discussed topics such as mind over matter, inner and outer space, UFO's, PSI, ESP, astrology, reincarnation, time, distant viewing, the energy body, auras, Kirlian photography, telepathy, pyramid power, etc. I picked the book up at the library at three o'clock in the afternoon and started reading it on the bus going home. I read it while I was cooking supper. I read it while I was eating supper. I took time out while my daughters were getting ready for bed and got right back to it as soon as I could. Around midnight I got into the bathtub and finally turned the last page. I had borrowed another book that afternoon so I picked that one up and finished reading it also before turning in myself. 'Psychic Discoveries behind the Iron Curtain' was 446 pages long and the other one just under 200 pages. The next morning before I went back into class I went back to the library to return the two books. The librarian laughed at me and said:

"Bit off more than you can chew, eh?"

"What do you mean?"

"Well you just took these two books out yesterday!"

"Yes, and I finished reading them yesterday!"

After hearing people telling me that I probably have no clue what the book was all about I was beginning to doubt myself. A few years later I borrowed the book again and this time read it very slowly. Well, I did not come across anything I did not remember from reading it the first time!

Back to School

When I came to Canada I was sixteen years old. We had signed a contract in Germany to work in the sugar beets for two years. Those were two very difficult years and when the contract had ended the difficulties had not. Learning a new language and settling down in a new country was really demanding, stressful and totally degrading. At age thirty-five I had an opportunity to go back to school. I was overjoyed. I had just finished registering and before leaving the building I wanted to go for a cup of coffee. It was a huge school. As I was walking down the hall I was thinking:

'I wonder where the cafeteria might be?'

A man was rushing down the same hallway about 50 feet in front of me, he turned around and pointed over to the right of me and said:

"It's right there around that corner!"

I knew I was not in the habit of thinking out loud. I was running a question through my head and he had perceived it and volunteered the answer!

Weird?

Just a little bit!

This man turned out to be my math teacher while I studied at that school. A few years later a famous psychic told me the two of us had lived through four or five marriage during previous life times. He had been a mathematician then also and at one time was in charge of building irrigation systems in early Rome.

"What about this time?"

"No, he has other things to do this time!"

"And so do you!"

One day Irene and I were sitting alone at a table during lunch break when our math teacher came over with his tray and asked if he could join us.

"So what are you ladies up to?"

Not having an answer ready I stalled for a few second by answering:

"You want me to tell you?"

"Jesus Christ, NO!

His face turned bright red – he was blushing – a man of about fifty years of age – blushing! Oh my God – I felt a surge of heat rising in my body and my face started to burn uncomfortably. I am sure my face turned as red as his – I was blushing too. We all started to laugh and spent the rest of our lunch hour chatting and laughing and having a great time. What had brought this on? I have a feeling he was experiencing a flashback that he could not quite explain to himself!

I enjoyed my math classes tremendously!

I made a few new friends and met our new teachers. I had a wonderful day and was looking forward to the coming year. As I was filling out a few forms that evening to get ready for the next day I saw a huge screen appear about six feet behind me above my head. It looked like a huge nine by six foot television screen. As I was watching I saw one of my new teachers write his name on a large blackboard. With his left hand! He was wearing a new looking, bright and shiny wedding band. It really sparkled! That was interesting! I had never seen that screen before.....

The next day as we were waiting for our teacher to come into the classroom my new friend told me how excited she was to get to know that handsome young teacher. I told her not to get too excited because that handsome young teacher is a married man! Of course she did not believe me; after all he was not wearing a wedding band the first day. I noticed that too but I knew better now. Well, the teacher entered the classroom, picked up a piece of chalk and wrote his name across the blackboard, in huge letters, with his left hand showing off a sparkling wedding band.

After that I saw that screen quite often. It was always silent. I never knew what was being said but every time the same thing would happen the next day exactly as I had seen it on the screen. These messages were to protect me and to prepare me when someone had bad intentions and was trying to hurt my feelings.

One day we had an in-class assignment in which the teacher told us about a half-page paragraph that we had to write down the way we thought the author would have written it. After listening to him I just sat there for about half an hour letting words and sentences run through my head. I picked up my pen and wrote down whatever came to mind. After the teacher read it he called me over and asked:

"Have you read this book before?"

"Do you know this author?"

When I told him I had never heard of him and had never read that book he pushed the book and my page over for me to read and compare. Was I pleasantly surprised? Oh yes! Absolutely! My page was almost identical to the one the author had written! Little surprises like this were happening all the time. Often when the teacher asked questions I would know the answer even before he finished asking it. A lot of times I had no idea what he was talking about but I knew the answer because he knew the answer. I would not hear anything; I just picked it up and knew!

Raised in a nest of Scorpios

No one in my family was interested in astrology. Ever since I was little I would look up my horoscope and pay attention to personality traits each sign represented. As I got older I realized I was growing up in a nest of Scorpios. My mother was a Scorpio, my brother Walde*mar* was a Scorpio, my brother Otto*mar* was a Scorpio and I, *Mar*tha am a Scorpio. Is it a coincidence Scorpio is ruled by *Mar*s? I just love how all of this fits together!

Astrology

I was very intrigued by astrology and studied it for quite some time. I got to a point where I could tell a person's sun sign after talking with them about nothing in particular for about ten minutes. I averaged about eight out of ten. The ones I missed were usually on the cusp or a few days into the adjacent sign. A few times I picked up on their moon because it had a stronger influence on their personality.

> *And there are those who talk,*
> *And without knowledge or forethought reveal a truth*
> *Which they themselves do not understand.*

> *Khalil Gibran*

One time we were looking for a table to sit down for lunch. The cafeteria was very busy and finally we found two empty chairs at a table that had about eight people sitting around it. We had seen these people in the cafeteria many times but had never talked with any of them. After about twenty minutes I heard myself asking the young man to the right of me:

"When is your birthday?"

I had not planned to ask him that and actually I did not need or want to know when his birthday was. He replied with a little surprise in his voice:

"You want to know when my birthday is?"

I did not answer but a little while later I heard myself repeating that question. Again he asked me if I wanted to know when his birthday is. Again I did not answer because I was getting a little embarrassed to have asked him that to begin with. I could not believe it but I asked him a third time. He looked at me for a while, took out his wallet, removed his drivers' license and handed it to me. Do you want to guess? His birthday was on that day!

On another day we were having coffee and were talking about astrology when a girl out of my class asked me if I could guess her birth sign. I laughed and said:

"That is easy, you are a Libra!"

She shook her head and told me she was a Cancer. We spent a little time defending our statements until she told me she was a premature baby. If she had been full term she would have been born two months later. That would have made her birth sign a Libra!

Go figure!

I have no idea what that is all about. I thought the birth sign was created on the day and time we are born. What does it have to do with the day we were conceived?

My crown chakra opened

After arriving home from a long day at school I collapsed on my couch for a little rest. I had a great day but was a little tired. I took a few deep breaths and noticed a spinning sensation inside my body. It became more forceful and worked itself up my body. I was becoming a little dizzy as it zoomed through my chest and up into my head. I had no time to think about what was happening. It whizzed around inside my head at a very high speed and shot out through the top of my head with a bang! I was totally amazed. I was not tired any more and felt full of energy as if I had just woken up from a good sleep. I felt wonderfully alive and free.

Distant viewing

I had joined a typing class and hated it. The teacher was banging two rulers together and shouting out the letters she wanted us to type. Behind her a metronome was making a racket and I became overwhelmed by all this terrible noise. I had just experienced a most wonderful weekend with a group of people from the Center of Positive Living who were studying the teachings of Isis and Osiris. We spent three wonderful days learning, sharing and meditating with each other and when Sunday night arrived no one wanted to say good bye to go home. Sitting here in this noise-filled classroom I tried my hardest to shut all this commotion out. I put my head down on my typewriter and imagined myself back in that room. I found myself walking around in the living room. No one was at home. I walked into the kitchen looking for the dog. I could not see it anywhere. I stood beside the fireplace enjoying the peaceful atmosphere when I was ripped out of my present moment and found my teacher shaking my shoulders violently shouting at me:

"Are you all right?" "Are you all right?"

"Do you want me to call an ambulance?"

Sending and receiving messages

Every now and then when we were a little bored with school work we would turn to our other interest and start sending mental messages to each other. The first time we tried it my new friend, Irene, would send the message and I was to receive it. We did not spend any time on details. At seven o'clock that evening I stretched out on the couch and listened. I did not know what to expect since we had never done this before. After a while I was seeing a swastika in my mind. I tried to shake that. This was silly. My friend would not send me a swastika. No way! I stayed put for about half an hour and gave up. The next morning in class I took out my piece of paper and put it upside down on the desk. She took out her piece of paper and put it beside mine. We both exclaimed in an apologetic voice that we did not succeed. On the count of three we turned the papers over to have a look. I had drawn a swastika and drew a line through it. Irene had also drawn a swastika and scribbled all over it to cancel it and below she wrote 'I am sorry.' We could not believe it! It had worked! We laughed and forgot to make another appointment for a few days.

Some time later another friend of mine, Rita, wanted to do the same thing so we also agreed for seven o'clock that night. I was receiving. A few months earlier I had designed and knitted a beautiful cornflower blue evening dress for her. What made the dress special was the multicolored embroidery around the neck trailing down to the hem of the dress. I loved that dress. It took me three weeks to make it.

As I was lying there listening I could see most of that dress but no embroidery anywhere in sight. Not even a single poppy. I assumed again I had failed and stopped trying. The next day I handed her my note explaining that all I could see was the dress without any of the embroidery. Sorry! Well I was pleasantly surprised. Her note said she was sending me the color blue. She thought that was the most beautiful blue she could think of using so she folded the dress up with all the embroidery folded to the inside. Then she sat down holding the folded dress on her lap thinking of me. Well done. I received more than she had sent.

Another evening we had made plans to 'send and receive' and again I was receiving. Rita had company drop by unexpectedly so she excused herself and went to the bathroom. She did not have time to prepare herself and as she was looking at the painting on the bathroom wall she decided to send me that. As I was trying to receive all I could see was a pond with water lilies sticking through a whole bunch of round pretty leaves. I saw a whole bunch of irises blooming on the edge of the pond. I saw some background but it was not very specific. The next morning we exchanged information and she told me about the people dropping by and she had to quickly pick something. I showed her my note. Rita was very excited. That was exactly what the painting looked like. The next time I went to her house she showed it to me. For sure! That was what I had seen that evening.

Uninvited Guests

They say that shadows of deceased ghosts
Will haunt the houses and the graves about
Of such whose life's lamp went untimely out
Delighting still in their forsaken hosts

Joshua Sylvester

Rita was a little psychic herself but did not put much value
on it. She told me that her grandfather, who had died many
years earlier, came to visit quite often. She could see him
every once in a while drifting through the living room but
did not appreciate his visits. She told me about another
problem they had been dealing with for some time! They
had a beautiful home with an unfinished basement. Rita
and her husband did not have a dog but every few weeks
someone's dog left a huge pile of poop on the basement
floor. They were really upset about that and getting tired
of having to clean it up. It had a terrible stench to it. I had
a feeling it was not a dog relieving himself in the basement

but perhaps it was the grandfather doing that to get her attention.....

After hesitating long enough I decided to share my thoughts with her. To my astonishment she was not upset and wondered if there was anything we could do to fix this. I slept on it for a few days and then told her I had an idea we could try. The next evening I went over to their house and the three of us sat down with a cup of coffee and made our plans. We were going to talk to her grandfather, each of us silently, and tell him that we know he is visiting and explain to him that he has passed over to the other side. Since he no longer has a physical body we are unable to see him or communicate with him. We told him he has a much nicer place to go to and his guides would help him if he allowed it. Rita would tell him that she loved him and missed him and that she wanted him to be happy and loved where he is now. When we could not think of anything else to say we protected ourselves and the house with God`s white light of protection and love and proceeded our silent conversations with grandpa. After that we talked to his guides and our guides and called it a night! That took about half an hour and we never mentioned the poop in the basement to any of them. Time went on and a few months later we ran into each other and I asked Rita about her grandfather. She told me she has never seen him around again and they never found any poop in the basement since then. Rita did have pleasant dreams about him once in a while and she admitted she silently chatted with him on a regular basis.

Living a Double Life?

Many years after my mother had died I realized I had a similar experience except I did not find out for many years. I was spending a lot of time with my mother. We were always alone. There were other people around us but no family members. I never thought of other family members. There were only the two of us. She looked like she was about forty years old. She was beautiful and always wore very pretty clothes that I had never seen before. Most of the time Mom was very happy and we did everyday things like going shopping, riding the bus to go downtown, walk around in the park or just hang out. We were never rushed and seemed to have all the time in the world. We enjoyed each others company.

Our get-togethers were always happy except once in a while Mom would be upset with me because I was not paying any attention to her. I did not understand that but did not make any effort to figure it out. At other times I wondered why she would not tell me where she lived. I wanted her address so I could go visit her or pick her up but she refused to give it to me. We both lived in Calgary but I had no idea where. It did not seem to matter. When we talked to each other our lips never moved and I never heard any sounds but that was of no importance to either of us. It seemed normal. At one of our meetings Mom was wearing a beautiful pale pink floral silk blouse and a perfectly fitting skirt. She seemed very quiet and after some time said:

"It's back! I am not going to make it this time!"

I did not understand what she was talking about but I had moments when I thought I knew that Mom had died of cancer years earlier and here she was alive and well. This happened quite often but I did not know how to deal with it because it drifted in and out of my consciousness leaving me a bit confused..... it was so fleeting that most of the time I barely knew it was happening. I asked her what she meant by telling me that it was back. She turned around and showed me her back:

"Go ahead, touch it. It's back! I am not going to make it this time!"

I touched her back and felt a huge hump under that silk blouse. Startled I woke up! I sat up and tried to figure out what was going on. This was the first time I remembered that I was visiting with my mother while I was sleeping! When I was awake I had my current busy life with my two daughters and I knew that my mother had died many years ago. I was in a state of shock! Who said life was simple? There was nothing simple about this.

In the next few days I gathered my thoughts and decided to do whatever I could to help Mom move on to the other side. I gathered that she did not realize she had died. She only lived one week after the ambulance had taken her to the hospital and now she was so heavily sedated that she was not capable of carrying on a conversation with any of us. She laughed and said funny things like 'what is that guy doing here with all those vegetables?' I assumed that she was living on the other side already and when she died there did not seem to be enough difference in her consciousness for her to notice.

For days I had conversations with her explaining to her that she has passed on and no longer had a physical body. I was not ignoring her; I simply could not see her from here. I told her about her guides and prayed to her guides asking them to please help her. I prayed to my guides. I prayed to God! I prayed to Jesus! I prayed to everyone I could possibly think of and asked for help. It worked because I have not visited with her since then. I don`t even dream about her. That upsets me some because I think I may have overdone the asking for help bit.

Still asking for help

One day I was at a meeting where several famous psychics were present. I told my story and my concerns about not hearing from my mother and not even dreaming about her any more. One of the psychics told me that she had been ready to move on when she showed me the hump on her back and told me she would not make it this time. Hearing that felt good to me. I was ready to bless it and let it go.

Wedding Invitation

Eleven years ago my youngest daughter got married. The wedding took place in Banff at the beautiful Cascade Gardens. I told my mother and invited her to come to the wedding. I really wanted her to be present. Teresa was only four years old when Mom had died and she did not remember her that well and I was sad that she could not have her grandmother attend this special celebration. Once all the guests arrived and the festivities began I had forgotten all about my Mom. The next morning when I woke up I was pleasantly surprised. Mom had come to the wedding. I sat there with a glowing heart reliving what I had seen. Mom held both my girls by their hand and the three of them were skipping from one cobble stone to the other to cross the clear water creek that ran through Cascade Gardens. Mom was quite young and my daughters were about the same age as they were when Mom had died. The three of them were laughing and giggling and really enjoying themselves as they skipped away. I only saw them from the back and they did not pay any attention to me. Teresa may not have been consciously aware that her grandmother attended the wedding but when I remembered to tell her, her face lit up.

My Gift from God

Two months before Jasmin was born I moved from Calgary to Victoria. I was really looking forward to having my baby. On the due date I went for my weekly appointment and my obstetrician told me it would be at last two more weeks. I was really disappointed. Two weeks was forever. I felt sorry for myself and went to a nice restaurant to give myself a treat. Banana cream pie sounded delicious and if I had to wait two more weeks I really deserved it. After I got home I got a stomach ache. It would not go away so I went to bed early to sleep it off. I was sure it was that banana cream pie. The next morning my stomach was still upset. I made myself a cup of tea and went back to sleep hoping it would go away soon. When I got up a few hours later my water broke. My stomach was no longer hurting so I thought I may as well go for a nice drive and enjoy the day until the baby comes. Of course I would drive by the hospital and see what they had to say about that. Well, they did not agree with me and checked me into a labor room. There were three other women screaming and whining because of their labor pains. I had no labor pains. Ever since the water had broken I felt absolutely perfect. No pain anywhere. The nurse gave me a sheet of paper and a pencil and told me to mark down the time whenever I felt a labor pain. Well, I did not want to upset them so I marked down a few pains. My doctor came by and examined me. No, my uterus had not dropped yet! No, my cervix had not started to dilate yet! Was I not in his office yesterday? Well, that was fast! I was told to take it easy and relax. The baby would not come for a long time. He would be back later that evening!

It was lunch time and a nurse came by asking me if I wanted a bowl of soup? No! I did not want a bowl of soup! I wanted to go for a nice little drive and enjoy the day! A little while later she was back delivering soup to the other patients. Wow! Did that ever smell good! I told her I changed my mind. Could I still have a bowl of Soup? Minutes later she was back with my soup putting it in front of me on my table and went to the back to roll up the head end of my bed so I could sit up and enjoy my lunch.

"Whoa!"

The moment I sat up my uterus dropped with a thud and I could feel my cervix gliding open over the baby's head, opening all the way up and pushing pains were hitting me one after the other. I could have thrown the bowl of soup back at the nurse. It was all happening way too fast. I called for the nurses but all they had to say to me was:

"Relax" "Relax – you have lots of time."

I kept on calling without getting anyone's attention. I started to hyperventilate. My lips turned stiff and I could not speak. Oh my God, here I was in a hospital and I was going to have my baby all by myself! I tried pushing my emergency button but my fingers had turned stiff also and I could not do that either. I was in an absolute panic. I felt the baby being born and no one was paying attention to me. I must have let out some weird sounds through my frozen lips because one of the nurses from the hallway came in and told me to take it easy. She was going to examine me to convince me I was doing fine. The moment she lifted the blanket all hell broke loose. The baby's head had already been born. I was quickly lifted onto a stretcher and two nurses pushed me down the hallway to the delivery room. As the doors swung shut behind us one of the nurses lifted the blanked and there she was - my brand new baby girl had been born in the hallway while I was being rushed to the delivery room! When I was lifted onto the delivery table and strapped in I was sure they meant to deliver another baby.

"Twins?"

I did not know I was going to have twins! Thankfully the nurses cleared that up for me. They were putting me up properly on the delivery table so it looked okay for the doctor when he came back. Thanks a lot!

My little baby was so beautiful! I called her Jasmin Ramona. The scent of Jasmin was my favorite perfume and I loved drinking Jasmin tea. Now I had another Jasmin I could love. The first few times the nurses brought her in for me to hold her big, beautiful eyes were not focused and were googeling all over the place. I just loved watching her. She was so innocent. I had never seen innocence like that and really did not know it could even exist.

Innocent and totally helpless!

Innocent, totally helpless and trusting!

Oh my God! That was a lot to handle! On the third day she was sleeping when they gave her to me. I placed her on my bent knees and watched her sleep. She stirred and opened her eyes.

She was looking straight at me!

She was looking straight into my eyes!

Straight at me into my eyes!

She looked like she was smiling! She looked soo content! I was so stunned! Did she recognize me? Her face looked like she recognized me! She was looking deep into my eyes letting me know everything was going to be okay. I could not move! I just sat there absorbing whatever was coming across from her. I just sat there loving her not realizing that a whole new world had just opened up for me.....

My other Reason for Living

Eighteen months later I was back in the hospital giving birth to Teresa. This was a totally different experience. I had worked full time managing a restaurant and quit that job on Friday afternoon. That Saturday I shampooed our living room carpet on my hands and knees, sewed and hung up a beautiful pair of living room drapes and made two sofa cushions to match the drapes. Did I mention I decorated the top of the drapes and cushions with end to end appliques. That alone probably took at least six hours to do. While I was doing all of that I was taking care of Jasmin and my roommate's little son who was the same age. Sunday morning I woke up with faint little stomach pains that came and went but were not uncomfortable. No one had to tell me, I knew I was in labor. My roommate took her son to Banff for the day and after her return I announced that if she had no plans for the evening I would go to the hospital to deliver my baby.

As our friends were arriving for the evening I was sitting in front of the TV watching the 'Dean Martin and the Gold

Diggers' and my roommate was doing my hair. The pains were getting a lot stronger and after the show was over my friend drove me to the hospital. Whenever the receptionist asked me a question I would hold my breath and finish answering the question after the pain had stopped. I was told I had to get upstairs if my pains were that close together and the registration had to wait until later. I told my friend he had to go home and I would call him as soon as the baby was born. I did not want him to hang around and feel obligated to hurry.

A doctor who had just finished delivering another baby was called back to look after me since I had not seen a doctor during this pregnancy. The nurses were upset with me because they had no medical history for me. I was given a bedpan so I could at least give them a urine sample. Well, my water broke and almost flooded the bedpan. Everybody was a little upset and I kept telling them to relax, I was not sick, I was only pregnant! Needless to say the moment the water had broken my labor pains were hitting me with only seconds in-between. I was made comfortable on the delivery table and a nurse stood beside me holding a gas mask in her hand telling me with a soft loving voice:

"This will relax you" "This will make the pain go away" "This will....."

I felt another pain hitting me and I heard myself shout:

"Well, then give it to me!"

I grabbed the mask and ripped it out of her hand and pushed it down on my face quickly taking a deep breath. It felt like I was inhaling thick honey. The nurse was trying very hard to get the mask away from me but I held on. The only thing I could think of was that no one had ever died from inhaling this gas so I quickly took another deep breath. Instantly the delivery table, doctor and all the nurses shot across the delivery room to the other side. I was left behind and I was watching somebody have a baby. There was a lot of laughing going on. It seemed a lot of fun but I did not seem to be a part of it until someone put a baby up against my face. I cuddled up against her face and rubbed my cheek against hers.

"This is my baby?"

I felt so wonderful. I drifted away until some time later I woke up in the recovery room. The nurse told me it was all over. I had a baby girl. Of course I did not believe her and kept telling her:

"Any moment now I will have another pain!"

She put my hand on my stomach to show me it was flat but I was sure that I would get another pain any moment now. After arguing with her some more I fell asleep again. Later that evening the nurses told me I was a riot! I was telling jokes and kept everyone laughing while the baby was being born. The next day all the nurses came by to meet me. Apparently they had never heard of anyone having a baby and watching the birth at the same time while keeping the doctor and nurses in stitches. I had felt no pain. I did not even realize that I was watching myself giving birth to my baby!

The birth happened at nine thirty in the evening. I had checked myself in at the hospital half an hour earlier.

Totally delighted

Teresa was a total delight! The day I brought her home Jasmin fell wholeheartedly in love with her. She spent every waking moment adoring her. When I put Teresa down for a nap Jasmin would stand beside the crib and watch her baby sister sleep. She always put her little hand through the side of the crib and gently placed her fingers on Teresa's cheek or forehead. Sometimes she would just stand there holding her hand. She would stand there forever just watching her sleep. I so loved my two little girls.

Teresa never cried. When she was three months old I put her up in her little recliner and placed her on the couch to watch me run back and forth tidying up the house. I had a laundry basket under my arm when I heard her call:

"Mama"

I was quite impressed. It sounded like she just said 'Mama.' Of course she was only three months old. Good try! Moments later I walked by in front of her again and again she said:

"Mama"

Oh wow, she made the same sound twice! I gave her a wave and a big smile and disappeared in the laundry room. The third time I rushed through the living room she called out with a loud, impatient voice:

"Mama"

Oh my God! She was looking straight at me! She just called me 'Mama' and I did not know! I thought she was just making sounds that sounded like 'Mama!' I dropped the laundry and grabbed my baby. I held her and hugged her and felt soo guilty I could not stop crying. After that she always called me 'Mama.' When Teresa was about nine months old she talked in sentences. Clearly and precisely, like an adult.

We had a family get-together at my brother's house and were watching family movies in the living room. There were a lot of children sitting and playing on the floor and Teresa tried to crawl across the room to sit on someone's lap. She stopped in front of my sister-in-law and reaching up with her hands said to her:

"Sit please"

Shocked to hear that Hanna looked at me with her mouth open. I shrugged my shoulders and nodded. Slowly she picked her up and put her on her lap. Teresa happily said:

"Thank you."

Hanna was so taken off guard she almost dropped her. Not only did Teresa tell her what she wanted, she was also polite. She was such a happy baby. I could wake her up from a deep sleep and the moment she opened her eyes she would have the biggest smile on her face.

All done

We did not have any disposable diapers at that time and potty training started when they were old enough to sit. The first time I put Teresa on her potty she had no idea what it was for. She proudly sat on her little throne and showed off until I took her off. The next time I picked her up from her nap and put her back for the next try I could not stay with her because I had something cooking in the kitchen and could not leave it unattended. I asked Jasmin if she could sit down with Teresa and explain what she needed to do and minutes later Jasmin called me to let me know Teresa was done.

"Oh really? What did she do?"

"Both Mommy!"

Oh my! Did we ever have a potty party. We danced around the potty and kept telling Teresa what a wonderful job she had done. From that day on Teresa was potty trained. If I forgot to remember Teresa would tell me she had to go. She was six months old.

Many times we rode the bus. Jasmin would sit by the widow and I would hold Teresa on my lap. She had a low and strong voice and always had something to chat about. Bus rides take a long time and can get boring and after listening to the happy chatter people would turn around to see where it was coming from. It never failed – they were always looking at Jasmin and were puzzled because they did not see her lips move. No one ever looked at Teresa. She was a baby and no one expected her to be talking!

Hysterectomy

About eight years later I was diagnosed with cancer and needed a hysterectomy. I had the best surgeon in Calgary and could not wait to get this behind me as soon as possible. While I was going under my surgeon was standing beside me gently squeezing my arm and telling me over and over again that 'Everything is going to be okay.' 'Everything will be all right!' 'You will be just fine.' I was in great hands and very relaxed. Half way through the surgery I woke up! I was in excruciating pain! It felt like I had a huge red-hot coal in my stomach. I tried to brace myself against that pain but was afraid my body would burst or I would go into shock. I tried to open my eyes and lift my hands to let them know I was awake. Nothing worked. I could feel the tube inside my throat touching my vocal cords but I was unable to move a muscle or make a sound. I knew the doctor would finish the surgery whether I was awake or not so I had to handle this quickly and the best way I could.

I realized that I had often experienced immense pain like this while dreaming and when I awoke everything was all right. That pain had never left any damage on my body. Immediately I told myself I am in a dream and the pain is not real. I repeated again and again 'I am in a dream - the pain is not real!' 'I am in a dream - the pain is not real!' After saying that about eight times my body slipped over to the left and got stuck on the edge of my body below me. The pain had disappeared completely. I lay there observing the surgery. I could see and feel the doctor completing the cut around the uterus and pulling it out of my body. When he was stitching things up it felt like birds pecking and pulling at my insides but I felt no pain and no stress. I giggled to myself and was quite proud because I was actually observing my own hysterectomy! After a while I lost consciousness and fell asleep again.

The next day I told the doctor what had happened during the surgery and he admitted that what I had told him was correct. I did not completely leave my body I just experienced a by-location.

The lady has aui aui

Jasmin was about three years old. We were riding the bus and she noticed a little black boy sitting in the seat in front of her. She pointed at him and urgently told me 'ba ba' 'ba ba.' I quieted her down and told her how sweet he was but she would not agree with me. She was very neat and ever since she started to crawl she picked up every little bit of debris she found on the carpet. I certainly did not know her idea of cleanliness included skin color and was at a total loss. A few weeks later I was shopping at Sally Anne's and there on a heap of toys lay little Timmy. Little Timmy was a soft rubbery black baby doll about ten inches tall. He had no hair but his head definitely had an afro hairdo. He was naked and quite dirty. He was a perfect little baby doll! I loved him! I took him home, gave him a bath and croched him a soft white baby outfit. Happily I presented Jasmin with my newly found treasure but she totally rejected him. She did not want to have anything to do with him and she really loved dolls. I did not want to push it so I treated Timmy like he was my own baby. My own little chocolate baby! I would cuddle him and carry him around with me and when I needed to sit down to get some work done I would place him beside me. This went on for a few weeks and slowly Jasmin got used to having him around and started to play with little Timmy herself. Wow!

Time went on and we were on the bus again sitting on the front seat facing the seat along the wall. A black lady was sitting there with a cast on her leg. I was not paying any attention to that until Jasmin pulled my arm and sadly told me:

"Mommy, that chocolate lady has aui aui!"

I was not prepared to hear that but immensely overjoyed once I realized what was taking place here. I hugged my little sweetheart and repeated what she had just told me while trying to keep my face dry:

"Yes Sweetheart, you are right!" "The chocolate lady has aui aui!"

The chocolate lady rummaged around in her purse, took out a handkerchief, dried her face and asked me if she could give Jasmin a handful of candies?

"What do you think of that?"

I still get choked up every time I think about that and after all these years Jasmin still has little Timmy!

My Grandmother

My Grandmother's birthday was coming up and I sadly realized that I had never made her a birthday card. If she had lived until now she would be one hundred thirty-three years old. I never dreamed of her and often wondered if she is happy where she is now. After I finished the card and printed it out I put it on my coffee table, lit a candle and read it to her:

> "Perhaps they are not stars in the sky
> But rather openings where our loved ones
> Shine down to let us know
> They are happy!"

This was absolutely perfect! A few weeks later I went to the Sunday Service at the Spiritual Center. We had a guest speaker doing the service and to my surprise she had a message for me. My Mother and Grandmother were coming through. My Grandmother wanted me to know that *they were happy and I should not feel sad about their past. The life she has had way back then took a lot out of her and all that cooking and feeding was more than she could cope with.* This was totally unexpected. She had actually heard me read her birthday card to her and I am grateful she shared that with me because it will help me to let it go now.

In 1914 my grandmother and her eight children were taken to Siberia, east of the Ural Mountains. Her oldest son was fourteen years old and the youngest child, a girl, was only four. My mother was eight years old and went to work as a maid and babysitter. Times were extremely hard. Eight years later they were allowed to return to Poland. Seven of my mother's brothers and sisters had died of starvation by now and my mother and grandmother were the only two family members to return home.

The train stop was located outside of town and the train was several days late arriving. All the people waited around outside until the train arrived because no one wanted to miss their opportunity to finally be able to leave Siberia. At one time my mother wanted to go back to town to see if she could find some food. They had not eaten anything for eight days straight and the last meal the living family members had was one boiled potato they all shared. It was winter time and terribly cold at this time. The roads were icy and slippery and my mother felt too weak to walk back to town so she took an empty water bucket to lean on and pushed her way back to town and then back to the train stop again. The train arrived the next day. All the people that had made it this far were given food and drink before they crashed for the night. My mother's face and jaw hurt so much when she tried to drink her glass of milk that she gave up after drinking only half of it. In the morning a lot of the people who had eaten as much as they could handle were found dead. Their bodies were too weak and unable to digest the amount of food they had eaten.

Would that you could live on the fragrance of the earth,
And like an air plant be sustained by the light.

Khalil Gibran

Souvenirs from Siberia

My mother had a lot of frost bite all over her body. Her right arm had several scars a few inches in diameter and her thumb was a lot shorter on the right hand with a big scar at the lower knuckle. Her largest scar was across her right rib cage. The frozen muscles deteriorated and when the wounds started to heal the skin attached itself right to the bone. At one time her mother took her to a doctor to help her with all the frostbite. After having a look at the sores the doctor told them the only help he could offer was to amputate her right arm. My mother could not stand the thought of losing her arm and ran out of the doctor's office. She decided to heal her wounds herself and gathered walnut leaves, rolled them with a rolling pin until they were soft and juicy and bandaged them onto all her wounds. She did this again and again and in time the open wounds started to drain and to heal and the only remains were those huge deep scars.

My grandmother never talked about her past. She was too traumatized about watching seven of her eight children die of starvation without being able to do anything about it. I can see that it took a lot out of her and am extremely thankful to her for telling me she is doing fine now.

Why?

A few years after returning to Poland another incident took place that traumatized my grandmother so utterly that she was never able to talk about it. My mother and grandmother walked to a neighboring town to visit two lady *friends* of theirs. After a lovely visit it was time to return home but the two women insisted my mom and grandmother stay and have supper with them. Even though they did not think it was a good idea and they should get on their way they did not want to be rude to them and accepted the invitation. As they were sitting around the dinner table about ready to start eating my grandmother noticed a black hair lying straight across her plate. She did not want to draw attention to it and thought she would just remove it and carry on like nothing had happened. Just as she reached for the hair it disappeared! She was at a loss and did not quite know what to make of it but ate her dinner before leaving to go home.

My grandmother did not feel well and got seriously ill the next day. She had a violent headache and could not stop throwing up. Her pet dog came running over to her and started licking some of the vomit and immediately started howling and ran out of the house. A few days later they found her dog dead in the barn. It had crawled into a corner and dug himself into a pile of straw. The skin on his head had cracked all the way open. My grandmother did not get much better and went to a woman who reversed spells that were put on people by others. The treatment worked to a degree but my grandmother never totally got over it and had headaches until the day she died. If her pet dog had not done what it did my grandmother would have died from that curse.

There were a lot of people living in Poland doing magic and witchcraft. My mother often told us about them. The story I used to like best was about one of Mom's neighbors. He had a big garden around his house and several fruit trees growing in it but the garden had no fence. At one time two teenage boys were walking by his house and could not resist those awesome apples on the trees. They picked as many as they could stuff into their pockets and wanted to continue with their journey except they could not get out of the garden. There was no visible fence but they kept bumping into an invisible fence and no matter how hard they tried they just could not get out. The owner was watching them and let them sit in his garden until morning. After he lectured them on the detriments of stealing he took them by the scruff of their necks and pushed them backwards out of the garden.

Lost in Grandma's Garden

Many years later, I was six years old and we were living in East Germany at this time, we went to visit my grandmother. She had a wonderful garden and the moment we arrived I ran off to see her garden to sample all the berries only she had. No one in the whole world could have had berries like that: Gooseberries in any color imaginable, black currants, red currants, transparent currants, strawberries, raspberries, blackberries, blueberries ….. there was no end to all that magic. The berry bushes were way taller than me and as I kept running from one bush to another I came to the end of the garden and at the other side of the fence I saw a sight I could have never imagined in my wildest dreams.

A few meters down the hill there was a little river and a fairly large sandy beach. Dozens of adults were sitting around on blankets and beach chairs wearing shorts and bathing suits. Little boys and girls were playing in the water and throwing huge balls to each other and building sand castles. Some of them were wearing the cutest little bathing suits and some of them were running around naked. I walked up to the fence and grabbed on to it, sank down on my knees and for the longest time observed in astonishment what was going on right in front of me. I just had to tell my mother about that! I got up, turned around and headed home.

Home?

All I could see were fruit trees, berry bushes, berry bushes and more berry bushes. There was no house in sight anywhere! I panicked! I was totally lost in my grandmother's garden and started to cry on top of my lungs. I had never cried before and I think this was the first time I had ever been afraid. A little while into my hysterics I heard someone call my name. My older sister had heard me crying and came to rescue me.

I *still* love Gardens

A few years later, we were living as refugees in West Germany at this time, I had another unforgettable experience in my grandmother's garden. We did not have a garden where we lived but my grandmother's apartment included a garden and she allowed me to plant a little flower bed in it every year. I think I may have been about twelve years old. One summer the two of us were standing there admiring our flowers when a butterfly fluttered around between us and set down on my arm. I did not move and we were both watching it. After a little while my grandmother was looking at me and with a never before seen smile quietly said to me:

"God loves you!"

There was so much love in her voice! Whenever I see a butterfly I think of my grandmother telling me that 'God loves me!'

My first reading at the Nanaimo Spiritual Centre

My first Sunday in Nanaimo I found myself flipping through a Spiritual Magazine and found a place I attended for Sunday Service. After several visits I received my first message from a departed family member. The man coming through was carrying a piglet under his arm and identified himself as my father. That was a bit of a shock to me because I had not talked to him since we left Germany some sixty-one years ago. When my parents were first married my mother raised her first piglet and often told us how much she enjoyed that experience. The piglet became my mother's pet and followed her around wherever she went. My father holding the piglet did not seem that accurate to me but the comments he made convinced me that I was really listening to him.

As I was growing older my involvements with my father became more and more disrespectful. I was nine years old when he returned from France where he had spent several years as a prisoner of war. Instead of finding that our life would now improve we found that it was getting more and more difficult to cope. We were afraid to talk to each other because many times we caught my Dad listening under the windows and spying on us.

One day as I entered the hallway coming home from school I saw him kicking my mother in the stomach with his big army boots on. My mother collapsed and fell backwards against the wall. At that moment he turned around and saw me standing there horrified with my mouth wide open. He pushed past me and ran out of the house and did not come back home for a couple of weeks. No matter how much my mother tried to console me I liked him even less from then on and life did not get any easier.

Every year the farmers would announce which fields had been harvested so we could go out and collect whatever they missed. This fall my brother and I went out every day armed with empty sacks and backpacks and a bottle of water to collect as much wheat and rye as we could find. We never wore shoes during the summer so we walked barefoot across the stubbly fields, back and forth and back and forth and moved on to the next field and on and on every day until our bags were filled. Once we got home we would thrash the grain to clean it. My favorite memory of the cleaning process was with the bicycle. We would put a blanket down on the ground and put the bike upside down on top of it. One of us would turn the pedals and the other one would hold the wheat or rye into the spokes of the wheel. The grain would separate and fall onto the blanket and all we had left to do was flip the blanket up and down until the wind had blown all the debris away. If there was no wind we would pick the grain up with our hands and blow until it was clean.

Before long the two of us had gathered two hundred pounds of grain which was enough to get the family through the winter. We had made an arrangement with the local bakery that they would give us four large loaves of rye bread for one shopping bag full of grains. One day my mother asked us if we had been to the bakery lately because half a sack of grains had been missing. No one could explain it until I told her that some time back Dad had asked me to go to the bakery with him.

"Did you get any bread that day?"

"Yes, four loaves"

"Where did you go after you left the bakery?"

"To our friend's house"

"Did you have any bread in the shopping bag as you were coming home?"

"No"

Well, that explained that! My father asked me to come along the first time so the baker would accept him as a family member and after that he could get bread whenever it suited him. He stole the grains my brother and I had collected day after day to help us survive through the winter and gave the bread to his woman friend whenever they needed some. He was our father! Not supporting us was one thing but stealing food from his small children, food that we had collected to get us through the winter, and giving it away to another family was something I had a very difficult time dealing with.

One day my mother was up to her elbows in the laundry tub scrubbing our clothes when she noticed my father's coat hanging behind the door. Since she had not received any financial help from my father since his return from France she wondered if we would find any money in his pockets. She asked me if I could check his coat and all I came up with was a big pile of letters addressed to my father in France sent to him by this friend of ours. I opened the first letter on top of that pile and read it to my Mom. After a line or two of chit-chat it said:

"Your wife and children are doing well! You can come home now!"

The day my father returned from France my mother and that friend, who was a cousin once or twice removed from my father's side and was also a refugee from Poland, had walked to town and were not expected to return until late that night and we were to go to bed and not wait up for her. As they returned home and turned the corner Mom spotted our house and saw all our lights burning in the window. Her stomach dropped and she let out a shriek:

"Oh my God, my husband is back!"

"I am sure you are mistaken! Why would you say such a thing?"

"No, he is back, I can feel it!"

As they reached the house my mother pleaded with her friend to come inside the house with her. She really needed her support at this moment. She declined! So her friend had been in contact with my father for a long time and had kept it a secret.

So here I was sixty-one years later and my father was making an effort to talk to me. I had no expectations and had no idea what he needed to say to me. In fact, I was surprised to even hear from him. After he told me about the many difficulties I experienced after arriving in Canada and the way I dealt with the never-ending problems I was facing, he admitted that he would not have been able to handle things the same way. He said he 'just did not have it in him' to deal with problems, any problems! He admitted that he was a shit-head of a father and told me how impressed he was by the way I managed to look after myself and that he was very proud of me!

He was proud of me!

I was soo moved to hear my father express such sentiments that I had a hard time making it home before breaking up in tears.

> *Tears are God's gift to us.*
> *Our holy water.*
> *They heal us as they flow.*

> *Rita Schiano*

A few days later I had my head on straight again and decided it was time for me and my father to have another chat. This time I was going to talk and he was going to listen. I lit a candle, turned on some soft music and made myself comfortable on my couch.

Wait a minute, something is missing......

I got up and fixed myself a drink - vodka, vodka, vodka and orange juice! O.K. This was perfect! I started by thanking him for talking to me at the Center and told him I accepted his apologies but that there were hundreds of things I had to talk to him about and that he was going to sit still for now because I was no longer afraid to express myself to him!

This took about two or three hours and before I went to sleep that night I knew we both had made good progress. A few days later I could not help but smile at myself - fixing myself that drink was not for me - my father had been an alcoholic. Did that drink make it more comfortable for him to listen to me.....

My father's father

We have always been told to accept people as they are. I did not like my father's behavior but told myself he lived the way he did because he did not know any better. Children learn what they see while growing up and become what is modeled for them. I don't remember my grandfather but he seems to be around and is, unknowing to me, a part of my life. A couple of month after my father first talked to me at the Spiritual Center I was told I had another message coming through. A father, my father's father, had something to say to me. Surprised to hear that I listened anxiously:

"He did not get it from me!"

End of message.

Wow!

That certainly was unexpected! I was stunned to hear his father come through but ecstatic that he spoke up for himself and set me straight! I rushed home and lit another candle (no drink this time) to express my gratitude from the bottom of my heart.

You need to write that book

I really enjoyed going to the Spiritual Center. The messages were always interesting even if they were not meant for me. I was fairly new to Nanaimo and did not know too many people. This one Sunday we had a visiting speaker from Salt Spring Island do the service. As always we went downstairs after the service to have a snack and coffee and chat and socialize. A man crossed the room and came over to where I was sitting and put his hand on my shoulder saying:

"I need to talk to you."

All I could say was:

"By all means, I am listening!"

"You *need* to write that book!

I sat there a little startled – I did not want to be offensive but had no idea how to express myself politely. The man had such urgency in his voice. He had come across the room to give me this message and I felt he was not going to leave until I had understood it. I told him I had no intentions of writing a book. Ever. After receiving messages at the Spiritual Center people would ask me questions and as soon as I started to talk about some of my experiences they would just look at me and change the conversation or just walk away.

In the couple of years since I had come to Nanaimo I had met only one man who was intrigued by my conversations and he had no time to talk to me that day. I had been told by other people, people I had never met before, to write that book. I really did not see the point in any of this. I told the man beside me that I had thought about it several times and had made up my mind.

Publishing a book takes a lot of money which I really did not have to spare. He did not give up on me. He pointed out what people would be willing to give to actually know someone who had experienced what I have to share. He told me I need not concern myself with the publishing or anything connected with any part of getting the book out. The only thing that concerned me was the actual writing.

Just write the book.

I tried to put the conversation out of my head but was unable to do so for a couple of years. It started to bother me until one day last summer when I sat down by my computer and seriously started to write. I wrote chapter after chapter and got more excited every day. Whenever I got stuck I would go back to the beginning of my book and re-read what I had written. To my surprise I found myself sobbing – sobbing – deep in my heart feelings were coming up that I had never acknowledged before. I was in awe. I needed to find out *who* the man was who had given me that talk at the Spiritual Center that started all of this. I found out his name is James Spencer, the Wave Walker, from Salt Spring Island. Thank you James Spencer! You have opened a door for me that could not stay shut!

We exist forever one way or another

I don't believe that ghosts are
"Spirits of the dead"
Because I don't believe in death.
In the multiverse, once you're possible, you exist.
And once you exist,
You exist forever one way or another.
Besides, death is the absence of life,
And the ghosts I've met are very much alive.
What we call ghosts
Are life forms just as you and I are.

Paul F. Eno

In my early twenties I met a very special friend. I had just come out of a devastating relationship several months earlier and through him I was able to pick up the pieces and start over. For the first time, as an adult, I felt valued and special just for being me. He always treated me like a princess.

One of our dates I treasure the most is the evening he took me out to the newest dine-and-dance supper club in Calgary. I had designed a special red cocktail dress with a red petticoat and wore red shoes, red fingernails and a string of pearls for that dreamy evening. Our table was not quite ready so we were asked to wait in the lounge until we were called. He walked me up to the bar, put his hands around my waist and lifted me up to the bar stool, sat down beside me and gave me a kiss. People did not kiss in public and we could have sat down at a table to wait. He showed me off and was proud of doing it! We were together for three wonderful years until he had to go back to Denmark to take over the family business.

When I was about forty-seven years old he caught me unaware with a surprise visit for which I was in no way prepared! I was lying in bed, on my stomach, about to fall asleep when I woke up with a start. Someone had just taken a firm hold of my waist and tried to lift me up. I let out some terrifying screams as I raised myself up on my elbows to see who had broken into my bedroom. In a split second he had let go of me and moved to the head end of my bed looking at me with the most shocking look of disbelief! He held his hands up in front of his face to protect himself from me. I was paralyzed! I could not move! I could not speak! My heart was beating so hard and so fast I think I could actually hear it! By this time I knew that my visitor was not a physical being. His feet did not touch my bedroom floor and he was almost a foot above ground and seemed to be a touch transparent. I had stopped screaming by this time and instead I was yelling at him:

"Get out of my house!"

"Get out of my house now!"

I heard myself demanding to know:

"How did you get in here?"

"What do you want from me?"

"Get out!" "Get out!" "Get out!"

I noticed that his feet and the bottom of his coat were becoming more and more transparent. Our eye contact never broke and I watched his face express such shock and unimaginable pain that it still startles me. The rest of his body continued to slowly disintegrate and after what seemed to be forever only his eyes were visible.

His eyes were the only part of his body that I recognized. They were definitely his. The way he moved and touched me were definitely his. The rest of his body was definitely wishful thinking! My friend had been a very handsome, kind and gentle man with a charming mustache but for this visit he created a rough and tough image with a shaggy full beard that made him look like a lumberjack!

This experience had really terrified me so after he had faded away and I had calmed down a bit I sat up and tried to regain my composure. My first reaction was to leave the room just to get away from it all and sleep in the spare bedroom from then on but instead I heard myself telling him in a shaky, rather loud voice:

"This is my bedroom and I am not leaving it!"

and

"You get out of here and if you have anything to say to me, please, find another way to get your message across; one that will not scare the life out of me."

I kept on sleeping in that bedroom but for the next six months or so I never turned off the lights!

Some twenty-six years later, at the Spiritual Centre in Nanaimo, I received a heartwarming message from him. I was totally overjoyed! This time there was nothing to be feared and it confirmed that once we exist we exist forever in one way or another!

My Dearest Childhood Friend

When you part from your friend,
You grieve not;
For that which you love most in him
May be clearer in his absence,
As the mountain to the climber is clearer
From the plain.

Khalil Gibran

We had another guest speaker at the Spiritual Center when I received a message from my dearest childhood friend, Peter. I was very pleased but not surprised. Even though I had not seen him since we came to Canada in 1954 and we lost contact a few years later I always felt close to him. The message I received that Sunday was that he wanted to reassure me that he was always with me even though he was not able to be physically present. In the middle of the message the speaker stopped and asked me how long ago he had died. I did not know so I asked my girlfriend

in Germany to fill me in. To my surprise he was still alive
and doing well. I assumed he had died about ten years
earlier when I had the most astounding and most beautiful
dream experience with him. Apparently he is able to send
messages through psychics when it suits him – no need to
permanently check out of the body first.

The dream was totally real. It did not feel like a dream and
I have difficulties finding words to describe what we were
feeling and experiencing. We were about thirty five years
old. We were dancing. Slow dancing. His arms embraced
my whole body and my arms embraced his. We were very
close to each other and gently moving to the music. We did
not speak. There seemed to be no need to say anything
because we could directly feel and absorb everything in us
and around us. I was aware of every cell in my body and
every cell in my body felt the emotions of each and every
cell from the top of my head to the tip of my toes and just
as clearly every cell in his body – from the top of his head
to the tip of his toes. I could feel where our skin touched
with such immense sensitivity and was aware of what he felt
as if I was feeling it with my own body. I was aware of every
thought he had and knew he experienced and understood
everything I felt and thought. I was completely overwhelmed
by feeling how he reacted to every little fragment of thought
and touch that took place within me and knew that he
understood I felt how he reacted to me. I loved that we did
not keep what we felt and thought a secret from each other.

I dream of him often but most mornings when I wake up
I only remember bits and pieces of what took place during
the dream. Most of the time I feel that he is showing and
explaining things to me that I have never seen before and
don't quite understand.

My last summer in Germany I was helping out at his father's store and experienced the most amazing summer ever. I was used to working hard and having fun but I don't remember ever laughing as much as I laughed then. Every time we sat down at the dinner table it only took us a few minutes after our eyes made contact and we would start to giggle. We tried to behave but the giggles would turn into laughter and we could not stop laughing no matter how hard we tried. It definitely was contagious because everyone at the table would be laughing along with us and one of us would have to leave the table to calm down. We took turns removing ourselves from the table but many times we would start laughing all over again the moment our eyes made contact again. Many times we could not put a stop to it and with our stomach hurting one of us would take our plate and finish our meal in the kitchen. The same thing happened in the afternoons when we took our coffee break. This went on for several weeks until I moved to the neighboring town to attend boarding school. We were both fifteen years old at that time.

Two or three years earlier the fair had come to our neighboring town and we all had to go and see what was going on. I could hardly wait. I was planning to go with my friend, Peter, but at the last moment he told me he had to accompany a few of the local girls and could not get out of it. I understood quite well. I was not born in that village and nobody really liked us refugees. When we moved into that village after the war collapsed we cramped everybody's style and they had to put up with us whether they liked it or not.

I got on my bike and went to town by myself. The fair was interesting as always and it took most of the afternoon to see everything. We went from booth to booth and watched the clowns entertain whenever they came by. Peter and the girls were always in my sight, only thirty or forty feet away but they did not make any effort to invite me to join them. We all knew each other quite well since we were in the same classes since grade one. I did not mind, I was used to their standoffish behavior.

Peter was tossing balls to win a prize while we all watched and as soon as he had chosen his reward he excitedly jumped up and down and looked around until he spotted me. He dashed over to me grinning from ear to ear and took one of my hands and put his prize into it and pressed my fingers close around it. After he ran back to his companions I opened my hand to see what he had given me. It was a cupie-doll. He had won a cupie-doll and had given it to me. The last time I had a doll of my own was the day we left our farm in East Germany to flee from the Russians. That was about five or six years earlier and I don't remember playing with any dolls after that. This little cupie-doll was magical. If it had been made out of pure gold it could not have become more precious! I placed it beside my bed where I could see it before I fell asleep and the moment I opened my eyes it was the first thing I would see before I got busy with my day. When I immigrated to Canada I took my precious little cupie-doll with me and this time placed it on top of my dresser mirror.

Many years later after my mother had died my brother asked me what I wanted to do with all my belongings at Mom's house. Needless to say I was so exhausted, tired and heartbroken that it was a challenge just to get through the day. I told him to donate everything to the Salvation Army and of course, without realizing it, that included my precious little doll.

The first few years after the war were tough and we had to make do with very little. In art class I did my sketches and drawings with pencil because I did not have any crayons or water colors. Peter sat behind me across the aisle and one day he quickly stepped up to my desk and dropped off a handful of crayons. A little while later he would come back with another handful of crayons and take the ones he had given me earlier back with him. He would repeat this several times during every art class so I was able to turn in colorful assignments instead of black and white ones. This went on for several years until I became a proud owner of my very own box of crayons. I had never asked him to borrow his crayons, he just shared his with me voluntarily.

A big part of my photo album from childhood is filled with school pictures. To my sorrow all the photos I have of my dear friend are so small that I cannot recognize him and in time I forgot which of the boys I should be concentrating on. From that distance they all looked the same. I was always sad that I did not have a nice photo to remember him by and a few months after I received that message from him at the Spiritual Center my long-time wish was answered. My girlfriend from Germany had sent me a newspaper clipping from my far-away friend with a close-up of him and his beautiful wife holding photos of a bunch of hawks that were nesting under their roof. Coincidence? I have a bunch of bald eagles living in the trees across the street from me.

When I came home from the Spiritual Center after receiving his message I dashed into my living room and collapsed on my couch. I cried and cried for hours – not only tears of sadness – I also cried tears of overwhelming joy! Tears I could not seem to or want to put an end to!

The gift of laughter

A smile starts on the lips,
A grin spreads to the eyes,
A chuckle comes from the belly;
But a good laugh
Bursts forth from the soul,
Overflows, and bubbles all around!

Carolyn Birmingham

Shortly after arriving in Calgary I realized I needed to replace the needle for the record player my brother had given me as a Christmas present. I made a note of the name of the record player and had a good look at the needle I needed and set out to go to the downtown Bay store. The electronics department was on the fifth floor. I found the counter and told the young man what I was looking for. He asked me what number of needle I needed.

"Number???"

"I have no idea what number of needle I need!"

"I can pick it out. I know what it looks like!"

The young man turned around and opened two large folding doors that spanned across the wall and reached all the way up to the ceiling. There were several hundreds of tiny shelves mounted on the inside of the doors and hundreds of tiny shelves mounted on the inside of the wall displaying needle besides needle – I could not imagine how many needles I was looking at – probably a couple of thousand..... The young man turned around and looking straight at me waved his hand toward the display and said:

"Take your pick!"

I was flabbergasted! I just stood there in amazement staring at what was in front of me. This was so funny I burst out laughing hysterically. I could not stop laughing. I tried to tell the clerk I would go home and look for the identification number but I could not stop laughing long enough to utter those words. After trying to compose myself and realized I could not I just motioned to the clerk, waved good-bye and left. I made it back to the escalator, rode down to the next floor, walked around and caught the next escalator and on and on until I had reached the main floor. I was still laughing at the top of my lungs and people stopped and watched me as I made my way through the crowds. I reached the street and was wondering what to do. My bus pulled up and I thought this would be the perfect way to stop attracting everyone's attention. I got on and took a seat on the very back row. I was still laughing. The bus waited a few minutes and finally continued to the next stop. A few people had started to laugh along with me and a few stops later everyone on the bus was laughing – hard and loud – just like me! I could no longer hold on and got off the bus several stops before my destination and walked home. Once I got home I collapsed on my couch but still could not stop. I sat there laughing until I was totally exhausted.....

Can we stop our pain?

One morning I lifted two boxes filled with bottles of vitamins down from the upper shelf in the kitchen cupboard. I had to stand on tippy toes and felt a little wiggly. As I had pulled them half-way out the upper box slid towards me and dropped a bunch of glass vitamin bottles on my head and face. The largest one must have weighed a ton and landed on the bridge of my nose. I let out a screech to deal with the pain and could not move because I did not want to drop the other box. The pain was immense and I was sure I could not cope. A little embarrassed to be done in by a bottle I took a deep breath and screamed:

"It is only pain!"

"STOP!"

The moment I had shouted 'stop' the pain vanished! I stood there in amazement and after putting the other box down I went into the bathroom to have a look. The bridge of my nose was bleeding heavily but I still felt no pain!

This was educational – I had no idea we were able to control our physical pain with our mind!

A *quick trip to Victoria*

The last time I spent time in Victoria was in the spring of 1964. Fifty-one years have gone by. The only area I recognized were the government buildings downtown. I had to go to the Bay complex to apply for a passport. I realized I had passed that complex and made a quick right turn, drove a few blocks and noticed a blue parkade sign. Another right turn and I was safely parked on the fourth floor. As I pressed the button on the elevator a young couple rushed up to me and told me how lucky I was to get such prompt service. Laughingly they said:

"If I were you I would buy a lottery ticket. This never happens! You are very lucky today!"

After inquiring for directions they told me one block this way and four or five blocks to the left. You can't miss it. It was easy to find. Applying for the passport took no time at all and I was ready to head back to my car.

As I stood in front of the Bay I realized I had come out of another exit but was not alarmed. I headed down the street happy that everything had gone so well and became a bit alarmed when my parkade was nowhere to be seen. I asked for directions and ended up at my first parkade. No, not mine. I asked directions again and found out there were about fifteen parkades in the vicinity. Wow, I figured there may be two or three all-together. I kept walking but every parkade I found definitely was not the one I was looking for. It started to drizzle a bit and I was getting hungry and took a break. I was standing on the sidewalk again checking my map when a young man behind me offered to help me find my car. He lived in Victoria and knew his way around. We walked to all of the parkades marked on that map but still did not find the one I had parked my car in. It had gotten dark and we decided to call it a night. After giving the commissioner at the last parkade all the information necessary to track my vehicle over night we walked back to his car and he told me he would drop me off at a hotel. I felt totally indebted to him. I was sure I had kept him from accomplishing his usual tasks. Instead of just dropping me off he insisted on coming inside with me and introduced me to the clerk telling her of my unexpected stay over night and before I could thank him properly for what he had done for me he had vanished.

I had the rest of the evening to sort out what had happened to me. Never in my life had I ever misplaced my car. Never! I was at a total loss. How could I have been so careless – stupid actually? I was quite embarrassed and knew I would never tell anyone about this!

The phone rang in the morning – yes it was Aaron. He told me he had found my car. He thought of that one parkade we had not walked to because it had been too far away.....

He drove there himself to check it out. As I waited for him in the lobby I became quite emotional. This young man had a heart of gold and he showed up when I needed someone to lean on – this was far better than winning a lottery – far, far better! To top that off he had bought me a huge, most delicious looking bran muffin covered with all kinds of nuts, seeds and berries because I probably had not yet have breakfast. On our way back to the parkade I told Aaron:

"What you have done for me here was big, soo big, no one in my whole life has ever done anything like this for me, not ever....."

"I bet you do things like this all the time, right?"

"Giving directions and things like that, yes, but this was **platinum**!"

"Platinum indeed!"

I felt such joy in my heart! I was not sure if I should follow through but I heard myself asking:

"Do you believe that we all have guides who help us get through our blue prints when we need help?"

"Yes, I do."

I liked hearing that – I needed to hear that right now! I felt happy and needed to share what I had been feeling all morning:

"I have three guides. Their names are Meridian, Sarah, and Aaron."

"You are representing my guide Aaron!"

Aaron turned his head and just looked at me. No words were spoken. Actions speak louder than words.

"Thank you Aaron. Thank you with all the love in my heart!"

The reason I had to get a passport was a little unsettling. Without a warning I was presented with a huge dilemma that required some serious decision making. I needed help and knew the best place to get it would be outside of Canada. There was no doubt in my mind and after getting all the details sorted out I shared my plans with my loved ones. Opinions differ and I ended up with a few question marks where I had exclamation points up to now. I still had to do what I felt was the right thing to do but I felt a little bit let down.....

Aaron coming to my rescue proved to me I *am* on the right track. Simple things can quickly turn into turmoil but hang in there you can never tell how beautifully they may turn out in the end!

Listen to your intuition
It will tell you
Everything you need to know

Anthony J. D'Angelo

About the Book

Ever since I was a little girl I dreamed of growing up, falling in love, getting married, having a house full of children and living happily ever after. To my surprise the blueprint I was born with had other surprises in store for me. As the years went by one door after another opened and I learned how magically even the most devastating experiences fit into the large plan. I am grateful for having received every single blessing and challenge - they made my life absolutely awesome.

About the Author

Martha Schlender was born in Poland, grew up in Germany and came to Canada in 1954. Throughout her life she tried to sort through her many childhood memories and was told that some of those memories belonged to her oldest sister, Wilhelmine, who had died five years before Martha was even born. Needless to say this started a long and intense search which is shared in this book.

Printed in the United States
By Bookmasters